NASM Exam Prep 2019-2020

The Certified Personal Trainer Study Guide including 200+ Test Questions and Answers for the National Academy of Sports Medicine Exam

Disclaimer

The questions included in this guide are samples that relate to many points you may study when planning to complete the NASM CPT exam. These questions will not necessarily be featured in the actual exam itself.

The data featured in this guide is based on the official NASM CPT Exam Blueprint. The terms associated with the blueprint may change over time.

The points here are also reflective of the CPT exam. The terms and points covered in the exam may change with each cycle that comes along. Be advised of what you may come across in your studies as you study for the exam.

Table of Contents

Introduction

Being a certified personal trainer, or CPT, can be rewarding. You can help patients with workout and exercise routines, as well as many rehabilitation procedures and functions. However, to become a CPT you must complete the NASM CPT exam. The National Academy of Sports Medicine has established the CPT exam to confirm that people who want to enter the field are qualified to do so.

This guide focuses on the six main domains of the NASM CPT exam, relating to how the human body functions. This guide also includes a series of questions that you can use in your studies and your preparation for the exam. Your success on the NASM CPT exam is critical to your future in the industry. You will be capable of doing more with your work as a CPT once you have successfully completed the exam.

About the Guide and the Division of Domains

The NASM CPT test encompasses six individual domains, utilized to identify your overall knowledge of how physical training functions work. The segments are listed in order of how they are covered by the NASM. The percentages next to each domain name refer to the approximate portion of the exam that will be devoted to that particular segment.

Domain 1: Basic and Applied Sciences and Nutritional Concepts (17%)

The first domain focuses on understanding the natural functionality of the body. This includes a review of muscle movements, dietary considerations and how energy is utilized. You will also notice how the central nervous system (CNS) helps to control the body's actions and how certain cellular functions may develop, thus causing specific actions.

Domain 2: Assessment (18%)

The assessment segment refers to what you will do when analyzing a patient. This includes reviewing movement functionality, how well a person can make repetitive movements and an analysis of other vital signs. The general criteria for assessment may also be included in this segment of the test. Part of this entails understanding what can be done for certain patients when they experience specific issues, and how they should be monitored, thus allowing a program to be designed accordingly.

Domain 3: Program Design (21%)

The program that you design for a patient will entail a review of the types of training activities someone can participate in. These include balance, core, flexibility and resistance training functions, among others. The process of making certain modifications and adjustments in a program may also be noted in this segment. The training methods you can prescribe to a patient can be included in this segment. The methods will vary, depending on the program. Multiple principles are covered, including overload and variation.

Domain 4: Exercise Technique and Training Instruction (22%)

The techniques people use when exercising are included in this segment. This refers to providing clients with the proper instruction on how to complete certain exercises. The need to produce better movements and functions is vital to note. The exercise functions include working with warm-up and cool-down and managing a person's core and balance. Much of this entails both safety and effectiveness.

Domain 5: Client Relations and Behavioral Coaching (12%)

A proper relationship between the CPT and the client is a necessity for the success of a program. This program concentrates on communication standards, the development of goals and barriers to success. Strategies for changing a person's behaviors may also be covered in this segment. This includes help tracking activities, managing physical work and other functions that may help with improving the participant's ability to exercise.

Domain 6: Professional Development and Responsibility (10%)

The final domain focuses on how you can continue to build upon your work as a CPT. You will have to follow the proper standards for managing your CPT, working with certain established rules and limitations. You can follow points in this domain on how to grow your business, but this is all based on your ability to adhere to certain guidelines and standards for operation. This is a professional-based consideration, but it can be useful for when you are aiming to help people make the most out of their lives.

The six domains in the program should be studied accordingly in order to improve upon one's ability to complete the exam and to receive one's certification. This guide provides sample tests on each of these domains, in order to review your knowledge on what each domain entails and how you can benefit from your work.

The General Test Layout

You will have a sample test at the end of this guide. The test is laid out with the following sections:

1. 20 pretrial questions; these are not to be graded and are often used to identify how well the test may be planned and laid out in the future
2. 25 assessment questions, with a focus on how to review a patient
3. 25 technique questions on how to produce an appropriate fitness plan and what teaching techniques are right
4. 25 program-design questions on what to do when creating a workout routine
5. 10 nutrition questions
6. 5 questions on operating a practice and developing your business
7. 10 questions on how to produce a strong relationship with your client

All segments must be treated with care so you can get the most out of your test. All test questions include answers listed at the end of their respective sections. The answers will provide you with a detailed explanation on why a certain answer is correct. In some cases, you will get an explanation for why some of the answer choices offered are wrong. Be advised that the questions in this guide are not necessarily ones that will appear on the test itself.

Domain 1: Basic and Applied Sciences and Nutritional Concepts

Structures of Anatomy

The Three Keys of Human Movement

The concept of human movement may be defined through the following three systems:

1. Nervous – the central and peripheral nerves
2. Muscular – muscles, tendons and ligaments
3. Skeletal – the body's bone structure and joints

All three systems are required in order for the human body to be healthy and functional.

Nervous System

The nervous system focuses on the general ability of the body to establish communication. This includes the body's ability to manage various functions and to allow the brain to trigger certain actions and motions in the body.

There are three functions supported by the nervous system, each supported in different manners:

1. Sensory

The nervous system identifies sensory changes in an environment. This includes being able to analyze and review certain changes that allow a person to feel the appropriate senses. A motor or neuromuscular response must then be produced.

2. Integrative

A person must be able to interpret the senses that are identified. The body can make decisions about what has to be done in a certain moment, based on how the body functions.

3. Motor

The body's motor system must respond to the information that it collects from the sensory response. The patient's proprioception is vital to the development of a healthier response. Proprioception is a measure of the nervous system's ability to create a sense of awareness of functions in the body.

Central Nervous System

The brain and spinal cord make up the CNS. CNS controls how information moves along the body and how a person interprets that data.

Peripheral Nervous System

The peripheral nervous system (PNS) entails nerves that link from the CNS to the rest of the body. This may operate certain triggered functions as the patient moves.

Somatic vs. Autonomic

The somatic PNS focuses on the outer body areas and skeletal muscles. Somatic functions are all voluntary in nature. Conversely, autonomic actions are involuntary functions; these relate to digestive functions, heart-related actions and so forth. The autonomic subdivision may be divided further into parasympathetic and sympathetic segments. The sympathetic autonomic system increases activities in the body to prepare for physical activities. The parasympathetic system reduces the body's functionality in periods of rest.

Neuron Functionality

The neurons or nerve cells utilized in the nervous system are crucial for the transmission of data.

A neuron is divided into the following parts:

1. **Soma.** The soma is the body of the cell. This includes the nucleus that features the body's DNA, protein-building ribosomes and mitochondria needed for producing energy.

2. **Axon.** The axon is a cable-like material that moves nerve actions along the cell and towards the synapses.

3. **Myelin.** A myelin sheath, consisting mainly of proteins and fats, covers the axon to protect signals that move along. The myelin's surface allows the signals to move faster.

4. **Synapses.** Also known as synaptic terminals, the brain's synapses occur at the end of each neuron. Synapses allow neurons to move signals to other neurons or to larger targeted cells. The functionality assists in triggering certain actions.

5. **Dendrites.** These are nerve endings near the soma. These link to other cells and allow signals or actions to move to other neuron or other types of cells.

Motor vs. Sensory

Motor neurons are efferent neurons that transfer impulses from the CNS to effector sites. Sensory or afferent neurons respond to certain stimuli that a person encounters. The neurons then transfer nerve impulses from the effector sites to the CNS.

Other Features

- **Mechanoreceptors** identify distortion in the body's tissues. These include pressure, stretching, vibrations and other external mechanical changes or influences.
- **Joint receptors** respond to pressure in the joints. Any sense of acceleration or deceleration will be identified.
- **Golgi tendon organs (GTO)** recognize changes in muscular tension.
- **Muscle spindles** are proprioceptors that move information on a muscle's stretching functions to ensure the body maintains a sense of posture and physical control.

Muscular System

The muscular system refers to a patient's muscle tissues.

The system includes:

- **Tendons** are necessary for connecting muscle tissues to the bone and allowing muscles to generate force.
- **Fascia** is the outside layer of tissue that surrounds a muscle.
- **Fascicles** are smaller muscle fibers that are bundled together.
- **Sarcomeres** are the functional features inside the muscular system. Each sarcomere features myosin and actin. The compounds are needed to promote muscle contractions.

The Four Main Parts of a Muscle

The four parts are organized from the outermost section of a muscle to the deepest tissue.

1. **Epimysium.** The outermost section, the epimysium works as a border.
2. **Perimysium.** This is a connective tissue that surrounds muscle fibers.

3. **Endomysium.** Individual muscle fibers or myocytes are surrounded by the endomysium.

4. **Tendons or muscle fiber.** The inside part of the tissue is made up of dense white tissue. This is an inelastic surface that links muscles with bones.

Twitch Functions

Muscle tissues are found in Type I and II forms, depending on the twitching functions produced.

Type I tissue is a smaller slow-twitch form of tissue. This takes a while to fatigue and does not produce tension as quickly. The tissue has more oxygen and a greater mitochondrial density. These tissues produce less power.

Type II tissue is larger in size and produces tension as a fast-twitch tissue. Although this generates info quickly, the tissue fatigues quickly. The greater force also entails a smaller amount of oxygen delivery.

There are several added notes to review surrounding these functions and how well they operate and work within the body:

- **Contractions** – Type I fibers contract slowly. Type II fibers produce faster contractions.
- **Aerobic enzymes** – A higher number of aerobic functions are produced by Type I fibers.
- **Anaerobic enzymes** – Anaerobic functions are greater in Type II fibers than they are in Type I fibers.

General Movement Considerations

Certain muscles in the body are more likely to move than others. There are four categories within which muscles operate:

1. Agonist

An agonist muscle is a primary mover that is regularly responsible for the same functions.

2. Synergist

A synergist muscle promotes the same form of movement as what the agonist uses, although the synergist is not as powerful.

3. Stabilizer

A stabilizer keeps the joints in an area stable and lessens the risk of further damage.

4. Antagonist

The antagonist muscles relax to allow the agonist muscles to move. The specific muscles in a routine will vary based on the exercise you wish to complete.

Connectivity Functions

Motor units are motor neurons which link up to many muscle fibers. This helps to produce more consistent connections between the brain and muscles. Neural activation is required in order for motor units to work. The activation is the contraction of a muscle, as produced by the stimulation in the neural system.

Neurotransmitters

Neurotransmitters are used in the muscular system as chemical messengers. Such chemicals will move nerve impulses from one synapse to the next. The impulses will eventually enter muscles, nerves and glands, thus triggering certain physical responses. Acetylcholine is a prominent neurotransmitter. The motor neurons release the neurotransmitter in order to activate muscles.

Epinephrine, or adrenaline, is released by the adrenal gland. The compound is naturally used to treat allergic reactions, particularly ones that cause breathing difficulties. The neurotransmitter may also be triggered through various sudden actions, including cases where the body responds to stress.

Local Stabilization System

The local stabilization system (LSS) is linked to the vertebrae. The region entails:

- Transverse abdominis
- Internal oblique
- Multifidus
- Pelvic floor
- Diaphragm

The fibers in the LSS are Type I fibers with a higher density of muscle spindles. The fibers are required for supporting compressive functions, rotational forces and other intense actions within the body. Primary muscles support the development of intra-abdominal pressure while producing tensions in the connective tissues in the lower back, or thoracolumbar fascia. The muscles may also help in increasing spinal stiffness, thus improving upon how the muscles may be appropriately controlled.

Global Stabilization System

The global stabilization system (GSS) links from the pelvis to the spine. The GSS moves weight and pressure loads between the upper and lower parts of the body. This produces stability between the spine and pelvis and allows the body to stay stabilized. This also helps with controlling core muscles and keeping them stable during critical functional movements.

The region includes:

- Quadratus lumborum
- Psoas major
- External obliques
- Rectus abdominus
- Gluteus medius
- Adductor complex

Movement System

The movement system refers to the area that links to the spine, pelvis and other extremities around the body. The muscles are required for producing force in a concentric form or for reducing force in an eccentric form. The muscles also provide stabilization while in operation.

Areas in the movement system entail:

- Latissimus dorsi
- Hip flexors
- Hamstring complex
- Quadriceps

Muscular Contractions

Contractions are required in the muscles to improve upon how well the tissues in the body grow and how the body moves accordingly, without limitations. Acetylcholine (ACh) is required for ensuring muscles can contract. ACh must be released and then link up to receptors in the body. This improves upon how the T tubule that moves into muscle cells allows signals from ACh to move through.

The potential for an action causes calcium to release. After this, the calcium binds to troponin, thus allowing binding sites to start operating. Tropomysosin, which blocks the receptors that trigger contractions, must be blocked itself. As the muscle contracts, the tissue in the area becomes active and functional. After the ACh is utilized and the muscles are at rest, the tropomysosin is restored to its original location, thus keeping new contractions from developing. This keeps the tissue healthy and lessens the risk of further harm.

Skeletal System

The skeletal system is made up of the bones and other connective features throughout the body. The system is designed to protect the body's tissues and organs. The bone structures may be supported through weight-bearing exercises. These exercises that require people to lift larger amounts of weight may trigger functions within the bone structure which allow tissues to become stronger and healthier.

Bones and Other Structures

Bones are hard connective features that entail a dense organic surface made of collagen, calcium and phosphate. The axial skeleton includes the skull, rib cage and vertebral column. The appendicular skeleton features the upper and lower limbs, the shoulders and the pelvic region. The joints around the bone structure act as movable or fixed features between bones. The joints require regular protection to allow for stability within the body and to promote a regular range of motion. An epiphysis may also be found in the tissue. This is a part of a bone that is separated from the rest of the bone through a cartilage layer. The tissue supports the process for uniting bones through further ossification.

Remodeling Bones

Over time, bones have to be remodeled. This occurs as older tissues are removed from the skeleton through resorption. New tissues are then formed through ossification.

The process entails the following:

1. Osteoclast cells are formed in the bone structure to remove old skeletal features through resorption.
2. Osteoblast cells produce new tissues in the ossification process.

The body must have an appropriate combination of the two features in order for the body to feel restored and for the bone structure to stay sturdy.

Features in the Bones

Depressions may be found in the bones. These are flattened surfaces where muscles are attached to. The process on the bone is a projection that comes out of a bone and is another space that muscles can link to. Ligaments can connect to bones and support how bones are linked to each other. Ligaments do not have much of a blood supply and are slow to heal. For bones to be fully functional, the periosteum must form. This is the regular bone structure featuring a fibrous outside that muscles can link up to. The inside layer is delicate and is vital for the formation of new bone tissues. Bone marrow and blood are stored inside the patient's bones. The medullary cavity is the area inside the bone shaft where blood cells are formed.

Nerves Along the Skeletal System

Nerves may be found in the skeletal system through the spinal column. They determine how well the body is capable of managing various movement and sensory functions. The nerves are organized as follows, from the highest on the spine to the bottom around the pelvis, with each nerve focusing on certain functions within the body:

1. **Cervical** – supports the neck and shoulders; eight nerves
2. **Thoracic** – chest functionality; twelve nerves
3. **Lumbar** – lower back area; five nerves
4. **Sacral** – along the sacrum; five nerves
5. **Coccygeal** – the tailbone region; one nerve makes up the coccyx

Paralysis may develop in injured cervical nerves. The thoracic nerves may also be damaged and cause some difficulties with trunk control. The injury develops as signals are incapable of moving into certain nerves and functions around the body. Other nerves may result in back pains or slight hindrances in movements if they are damaged or worn.

Cardiorespiratory System

The cardiorespiratory system refers to the heart and lungs. The system may be divided up between the cardiovascular and respiratory systems.

Cardiovascular System

The cardiovascular system focuses on heart and blood functions; this includes how blood vessels work. The cardiac muscle is shorter than a skeletal muscle, tighter in its function and operates involuntarily. The key parts of the muscle focus on managing consistent functions in the cardiovascular system.

Blood Functionality

Proper blood flow is required throughout the body in order for a person to be healthy. Blood has three vital functions in the cardiovascular system:

1. Transporting compounds

Blood works as a carrier of oxygen, hormones and nutrients. All must be regularly transferred throughout the body in order for it to be healthy. Waste products in the body are carried by the blood to the lymph nodes, allowing the body to stay healthy.

2. Protection

The clotting compounds in blood are needed to prevent possible bleeding during an injury. Also, the antibodies found in the blood and white blood cells are required for controlling how the body responds to certain infections and illnesses.

3. Regulation

The blood also regulates how well the body's pH level, temperature and other functions are operating. A person who experiences blood loss will be less likely to have proper control over his or her body. This includes the potential for normally healthy tissues to die off due to a lack of blood in the region.

Atria

The atria in the heart are located on both sides; these are the left and right sides. The right atrium receives blood that enters the heart through the entire body. The sinoatrial (SA) valve is included in the right atrium to produce the impulses needed for the heart, thus controlling the heart rate. The SA valve is considered to be a pacemaker for keeping the heart functional. The left atrium takes in blood that comes from the heart through the lungs.

Ventricles

The ventricles are also on the left and right sides of the heart. These are larger than the atria and help in pumping blood out from the rest of the body. The right ventricle is thin due to how it takes in a lower amount of blood. The right ventricle focuses on managing blood to the lungs. Specifically, deoxygenated blood is pumped by the right ventricle and moved into the lungs. The left ventricle is a thicker tissue which handles a higher pressure level. The area produces oxygenated blood that moves to other tissues around the body.

Other Features

- **Arteries** are required for carrying blood away from the heart.
- **Veins** move blood back into the heart.
- **Arterioles** are small branches inside arteries that end up in smaller spaces (known as capillaries) that move out towards other parts of the body.
- **Capillaries** are the smaller vessels at the end of arterioles. These are where gases, water and chemicals are exchanged for added control within the body.
- **Venules** are smaller veins that link the capillaries to other veins.

General Measurements

- **Stroke volume** is the total amount of blood that is pumped within each heart contraction.
- **Heart rate** is a measure of how often the heart pumps; this is measured in beats per minute or bpm. An average adult should have a heart rate of about 70 to 80 bpm.
- **Cardiac output** is a measure of the blood pumped per minute. This is measured by multiplying the heart rate by the stroke volume.

Respiratory System

The respiratory system links up to the cardiovascular system to assist in bringing oxygen into the body while removing carbon dioxide. The system consists mainly of the lungs and passageways that allow air to move through.

Inspiration and Expiration

The respiratory system operates with two separate functions. First, there is the process of inspiration. This is where inspiratory muscles contract to allow air to get into the lungs. The inspiratory system is primarily made up of muscles like the diaphragm and external intercostals. The secondary system includes scalenes, the pectoralis minor and sternocleidomastoid areas. The expiration process involves the inspiratory muscles being relaxed while the expiratory muscles are contracted. The expiratory muscles are active and help with moving air out of the region. Expiratory muscles include the internal intercostals and abdominal muscles. These actions may be measured and identified during basic exercise routines. The actions may be reviewed to ensure the patient is not struggling with workouts. In some cases, a person's ability to handle these functions may be impaired due to prior illnesses or could be weakened due to age or from repeated impacts to the region.

Oxygen Consumption

The resting oxygen consumption, or VO2, is measured by multiplying 3.5 mL by 1 kg-1 and then multiplying that by 1 min-1 to get a single metabolic equivalent or MET. The maximum oxygen consumption, or VO2max, is the top rate of transport that can be produced in the body. The measurement is based on a person's peak of physical exercise.

The Influence of Exercise

The respiratory system is heavily influenced by exercise. A person who engages in regular physical activity will experience changes in cardiac functionality, with the system becoming more active and capable of transferring oxygen and other compounds through the blood. Fats are also used for providing the body with energy. An increase in respiratory functionality through exercise causes a sense of alertness in the body. The level of lean body mass may also improve based on exercise.

Exercise reduces a patient's resting heart rate and blood pressure levels. This may also reduce cholesterol levels over time. Exercise improves the body's ability to manage glucose and other compounds in the blood. This may reduce a patient's potential for developing diabetes or other related issues.

Endocrine System

The endocrine system focuses on the production of hormones needed for managing regular bodily functions and for keeping the body active before risking problems that might add additional stress to certain functions.

Note: Although the glands themselves are vital for maintaining the body's health, it is extremely difficult to measure actual hormone levels. The activity levels of individual glands may be seen in some tests.

Vital Glands

- **Hypothalamus.** The hypothalamus links the endocrine system to the nervous system. The gland triggers the pituitary gland to make hormones.
- **Pituitary.** This gland uses signals from the brain to trigger functions that let other glands know what should be done. Part of this includes regulating the production of human- growth hormone and many gender-related hormones.

- **Pineal.** The pineal gland produces melatonin, a compound needed to help get the body to sleep.

- **Thyroid.** The body's metabolic rate is controlled by the thyroid gland. Hypothyroidism may cause a reduced heart rate. Hyperthyroidism will cause the heart rate to become dangerously elevated and may trigger unnecessary weight loss by burning off some muscle tissue.

- **Parathyroid.** The parathyroid regulates the calcium and phosphorous levels in the body, thus improving upon how well the bone structures in the body can be supported.

- **Thymus.** White blood cells are produced here to improve upon how the body handles outside compounds. White blood cells are the basic building blocks of the body's immune system. The thymus is larger in children and is smaller and less productive later in life.

- **Adrenals.** Adrenaline, or epinephrine, is produced in the adrenals to control physical actions and responses to certain stimuli. The glands may also trigger metabolic functions in some patients.

- **Pancreas.** The organ produces digestive enzymes and insulin. These are required for processing nutrients and for regulating blood sugar levels, thus ensuring the body has enough energy for basic functions and exercise.

Key Hormones

- **Testosterone** is an anabolic hormone that produces male traits. It's more prominent among men, although traces can be found in women. The hormone is responsible for producing the muscle mass and bulk that a man has, along with triggering hair growth.

- **Estrogen** produces female traits. This is needed for triggering proper lean muscle tone, although it can also cause fats to build up around the hips, thighs and buttocks.

- **Insulin** is needed for managing glucose. This helps with breaking down glucose, thus preventing it from being deposited as fat in the body. Insulin utilizes the breakdown of glucose to provide the body with added energy.

- **Growth hormone (HGH)** is an anabolic hormone that is required for the body's growth. Accordingly, HGH is found mainly in children and is especially prominent during puberty. HGH levels substantially decline in adulthood.

Functions of Exercise Physiology

Nervous System

Motor Units

A motor unit is a feature in the nervous system where a motor neuron is triggered. As an axon enters into a muscle, the axon branches and forms added synapses that target other muscle fibers. Each fiber is linked to a single neuron. As the motor units start working, the action potential develops. This triggers the potential for added motions and actions. The goal is to allow all the muscle fibers to stay active and functional during the lifting process. Motor units are considered to be the focal point of the nervous system. It is through the nervous system that many sensations and physical actions are triggered. Failure among motor units may result in paralysis or a general lack of sensation in the body.

Action Potential

Action potential refers to electrical signals that are sent out by motor units. The new ions produced by the neuron in the motor unit allow the body to move from its resting state to an active state as it notices a change in the cell.

Voltage-Gated Cells

A vital part of the nervous system's functionality are voltage-gated cells. The cells open and close as the voltage shifts along a series of gates within sodium channels in the brain. Gate m is the activation gate. Usually closed, it only opens when cells develop a positive voltage. Gate h is the deactivation gate. Typically open, this gate will shut down when voltage is reduced or becomes negative. Gate n is closed and will open as the cell becomes very positive, or depolarized. The movement of ions through the sodium channels is vital for ensuring proper muscle contractions. This is vital for ensuring the brain's general functionality.

Muscular System

Sliding Filament Theory

Sliding filament theory states that filaments of various sizes will slide along one another. This causes a shortening of the sarcomere, the tissues in the muscles needed for promoting muscular contractions.

Muscle Action Spectrum

There are three major types of muscle actions that may be identified in the muscle action spectrum:

1. Concentric

The concentric process occurs as the muscle force produced is greater than the force of resistance. At this point, the muscle shortens.

2. Eccentric

The muscle produces extra tension while it is lengthening. This causes the force to be a little lighter in intensity.

3. Isometric

During the isometric process, the force from the muscles is equal to the force of resistance. The muscle therefore remains its same size and does not experience any changes in its length. The length-tension relationship directly influences how well the muscle can strengthen. The resting length of the muscle is measured with the tension produced at that length. A force-velocity curve may also be identified in the muscle action spectrum. When the velocity of a contraction increases, the concentric force declines while the eccentric force increases. A force-couple process may also be noticed when multiple muscles work together to generate the desired movement. A patient must attain neuromuscular and structural efficiency in order for a workout to be successful. Neuromuscular efficiency refers to how force is produced and then reduced. The kinetic chain is then stabilized to allow the body to remain stable.

Davis's Law

Davis's Law is a part of the muscular system that analyzes how soft tissues can handle certain demands. Injured soft tissues will heal in the manner in which they are stressed. Davis's Law says that the body's soft tissues will become elongated when tensions are added. Any ligaments that are loose will eventually shorten, but tissues that continue to be worked upon will continue to stay strong. The basic concept of Davis's Law is that the body needs to continue working on its muscles to allow those tissues to keep on growing and becoming stronger as they eventually heal. Muscles that are not worked out will end up weakening and will become harder for the body to process.

Allowing muscles enough time to heal is vital for the success of a workout. This may require a participant to focus heavily on rest periods in between workout sessions. Such periods may assist a participant in ensuring that the body is restored, reducing the likelihood of injury. However, rest periods should be timed to allow the body to recover and to keep any effects from settling in. Proper timing for rest periods in between reps will be covered later in this guide.

Inhibition

Autogenic inhibition occurs as neural impulses identify sudden tensions that are greater than the impulses that are causing muscle contractions to develop. This causes muscle spindles to develop. Reciprocal inhibition develops as one muscle and its accompanying antagonist contract at the same time. This may cause pain or a lack of mobility in some instances. Inhibitory concerns often lead a patient to look for the path of least resistance in order to build muscle. This refers to relative flexibility.

The Cumulative Injury Cycle

The basic energy cycle for muscles is as follows:

1. Trauma develops on a tissue.

Pattern overload may be a concern; this develops as a person places unusual stresses on the body. This includes repeatedly using the same motion incorrectly.

2. The impacted area develops inflammation.
3. Muscle spasms are triggered.

Altered reciprocal inhibition develops when a tight agonist is formed.

4. Adhesions start to form.
5. A patient develops changes in control over how his or her muscles work.

Postural distortion patterns may develop among some people. This is a pattern where the muscles are not balanced accordingly; this is often due to voluntary actions, although they may also be unintentional. Also, synergistic dominance may occur as a synergist replaces the functionality of a weaker tissue.

6. Muscle imbalances start to develop.

Imbalances occur when the muscle lengthens around the joint.

7. The issue causes further trauma to develop, due to the person abruptly changing exercises.

The sudden changes in how the body functions may cause damages that take a bit of time to heal. A proper workout routine ensures that the risk of further damages to the tissues is reduced and the body can restore its natural functions over an extended period.

OPT Model

The OPT Model is a reference to how a person can manage a workout. The process entails five phases:

1. Stabilization

The stabilization process requires a person to maintain postural equilibrium. The joints must also be supported at this point to ensure a proper sense of function and control in the patient's body.

2. Strength Endurance

The next three phases comprise the strength process of the workout. In the strength endurance segment, the participant contracts his or her muscles for an extended period of time, encouraging a healthy sense of movement.

3. Hypertrophy

Hypertrophy entails how the skeletal muscle fibers expand in size during a workout, particularly when engaging in resistance training actions. As the fibers expand, the muscles become more noticeable and stronger in intensity.

4. Maximal Strength

A patient's maximal strength is the largest amount of force that a muscle can produce in one motion.

5. Power

After engaging in strength training functions, a patient's power level may increase. Thus, more force is produced by the muscles in a brief time.

Skeletal System

Joint Functionality (Arthrokinematics)

The movement of joints is measured through arthrokinematics. This refers to the movements of the joints when a bone goes through its regular range of motion. An articular, or hyaline cartilage segment in the joint, is the connective tissue that links the end a bone that will produce a joint. The connective tissue has to flow together and stay soft and protected. Any failures in the area may cause the joints to wear out and produce a lack of motion. In some cases, a person might develop arthritis if the support structures in the area are not secure or if those points have worn out.

Synovial vs. Non-Synovial

Synovial joints are tissues that are held through a joint capsule and a series of ligaments. Such joints have the highest range of motion. Non-synovial joints do not have a joint cavity, nor are they supported by any connectivity tissues or cartilage. There are very few, if any, movements involved in these joints.

Motion and Joint Types

Hinge joints are common tissues that offer a sagittal plane movement. Part of this includes proper twisting motions in the body, to support various movements. These joints include the ankles and elbows. Ball and socket joints are designed to support roll, slide and spin movements in the body. These joints include the hips and shoulders. Such joints are highly mobile. The motion forms in these joints can directly influence how well the body responds to certain medical treatments. A person should be monitored to ensure that his or her workout is tailored accordingly.

Planes of Motion

Three planes of movement are utilized to manage basic actions in the human body.

1. Sagittal

The sagittal plane moves through the front of the body to the back. The plane divides the body between its left and right parts. Flexion and extension movements are included in this plane. Part of this includes moving the body forward and backward while still in the same position. For instance, a person who participates in squatting exercises is moving in a sagittal plane of motion.

2. Frontal

The frontal plane refers to sideways movements, known as abduction and adduction actions.

3. Transverse

A transverse movement entails rotational movements. The plane is found in the middle part of the body and is parallel with the ground surface. Examples of transverse motions include things like swinging a bat or golf club. Throwing actions may also be considered transverse motions. The movement is the most complex due to the diverse nature of the motions involved and the variety of muscle features that may be triggered.

Basic Types of Joint Motions

The joint motions that a person might encounter include the following:

- **Flexion.** The body bends as the flex decreases in intensity between segments.
- **Extension.** The body straightens where the angle at the joint is increased in intensity.
- **Plantarflexion.** The ankle is extended in its position.
- **Dorsiflexion.** The ankle flexes in position.
- **Abduction.** The movement in the body goes away from the middle. Moving one's fingers away from each other while stretching the hand outward is an example of abduction.
- **Adduction.** The movement produced goes toward the middle.
- **Horizontal abduction.** The transverse plane movement goes from the anterior to lateral position.
- **Internal rotation.** The body rotates towards the midline. The rotation can entail any part of the body.
- **External rotation.** The body rotates outward past the midline.

Such motions may be observed in most joints. When planning a routine, you must assess how well a person can move these joints. Part of this includes ensuring that a joint is not at risk of wear or damage due to repeated use.

Endocrine System

Hormone Concentration

Hormone concentration in the body is heavily determined by how hormones are produced. The rate of production involved may influence how well the body can manage exercise functions. The rate of delivery is also vital to note. The rate refers to blood flow into an organ or other targeted cells. When the blood flow is high, the body's ability to move hormones is improved. This is one reason why managing blood pressure is so critical to good health.

Feedback Control

Feedback control in the endocrine system refers to how well the system can integrate itself with the nervous system. The nervous system may potentially influence the production of hormones, depending on how the body is functioning in a workout. When experiencing an immense amount of stress, for instance, a patient may develop a higher glucose level.

There are three feedback control functions to observe in the body:

1. Humoral

The humoral response occurs as glands respond to chemical levels within the blood. The parathyroid gland may respond to cases where blood calcium levels are low.

2. Neural

A neural response takes place as glands release hormones after nerves are stimulated. Adrenaline may be produced in cases where a person is in a highly intense situation.

3. Hormonal

Hormonal control occurs as glands produce hormones after they are stimulated by other hormones.

Responses to Exercise

A feedback loop may be produced as the body responds to exercise motions. Positive or negative feedback may be developed to either reinforce or counteract an action.

Cellular reactions, in this case, entail the following steps:

1. A receptor receives a stimulus.
2. A sensory neuron carries an impulse from a receptor to the integration system.
3. The integration system or center links sensory data to motor neurons through synapses supported by the CNS. Many signals are monosynaptic, as the synapses involved directly link to one another. A polysynaptic response may also occur if there are other neurons present in the process.
4. A motor neuron carries the impulses that were produced and transports them to the effector.
5. The effector is where the patient responds to the stimulus.

The cellular reactions that are produced cause a reflex to occur. This may cause the body to change its position, or a person will respond differently to certain functions or actions in a workout.

Cardiorespiratory System

Respiratory Pump

The respiratory pump is vital for ensuring that the lungs can handle natural expansion and contraction processes.

1. As the patient inhales, the thoracic cavity expands in size.
2. The pleural cavities develop less pressure.
3. Air is moved into the lungs. Blood is also brought into the area.
4. As the patient exhales, the pressure within the pleural cavities starts to increase again.
5. Blood is moved into the right atrium.

Through the regular process, it becomes easier for the body to respond to a workout routine. Accordingly, the body will have an easier time managing natural breathing functions.

Digestive System

Any digestive actions within the body are slowed down during a workout routine. As a person exercises, the energy regularly used for digestive functions will be utilized for processing blood so it may move into the muscles and lungs. As a result, it's best not to eat right before a workout, or a person may experience gastrointestinal distress, heartburn or vomiting. For the best results, a person should consume foods that are high in carbohydrates and low in fats before working out. These foods are digested faster by the body. Proteins, fiber and other foods that take a longer time to digest should be avoided. Hydration is possible during a workout, but a person should take large gulps of water to allow the fluid to get out of the stomach at a faster rate. This effort will help to alleviate any discomfort a patient may be facing.

Bioenergetics and Exercise Metabolism

Bioenergetics refers to the study of energy in the body. This includes how the body takes in that energy and what it does to utilize the energy that is generated in any function. The processes vary based on the components needed for proper functionality.

Anaerobic vs. Aerobic

Anaerobic and aerobic energy can be utilized within the body. The processes vary based on how much oxygen is used. Anaerobic functions do not require oxygen. The exercises involved are often high in intensity. Aerobic activities require oxygen. Such exercises are intense and require additional energy for long-term workouts.

Energy Systems

The three energy systems are used in order. The second system may work when the first system has run out, and the body has used enough of a certain compound.

1. ATP-PC

Adenosine triphosphate, or ATP, is a unit within cells that assists in storing and transferring energy. Phosphocreatine, or PC, may also be utilized for managing energy functions in the body. The system works as an anaerobic function that does not need oxygen. Anaerobic exercises may be conducted in the ATP-PC energy process. The exercises are to be intense and can work for about 10 to 15 seconds at a time. High amounts of power are produced for a shorter period. ATP-PC exercises include sprinting short distances and lifting heavy weights for about three to five repetitions. ATP may be converted into adenosine diphosphate. This will transfer energy around the body during glycolysis.

2. Glycolysis

Glycolysis refers to how well glucose can be broken down. This is a longer energy system than the ATP-PC process, as it focuses on allowing glucose to be utilized and prevents possible fat deposits from forming. The exercises in the glycolysis system are also intense, although they can be slightly lighter in intensity if one wishes. A mid-level run of about 200 to 800 yards is a process that focuses on glycolysis. Glycolysis must be observed cautiously as, while more power can be produced, the pyruvic acid that is produced will be converted into lactic acid, fatiguing the body.

3. Oxidative

The oxidative process entails low-powered exercises over an extended period of time. In this, the Krebs cycle occurs as glucose that was used in glycolysis stays oxidized, while more ATP is formed to allow energy to move through. Enzymes also move into the electron transport chain. Hydrogen combines with oxygen, and water is generated to produce a proper amount of action. Acidity is also prevented in the process. Triglycerides and carbohydrates are properly metabolized to create ATP. This works through lipolysis, which causes all fats to be metabolized just like the carbohydrates one consumed earlier.

Excess post-oxygen consumption, or EPOC, should be measured after exercise. This is a measure of how the body's metabolic rate has increased following the workout. Beta-oxidation can also occur as fatty acids wear out. Beta carbons in the acids will oxidize while two-carbon segments from fatty acids are also lost. These changes cause the body to handle more burn-off functions.

Metabolic Functions

Metabolism refers to the processes in the body, both chemical and physical, that allow materials to be produced and burned off. The process helps with generating energy within the body. Substrates are substances processed by enzymes in the body. The basic processes ensure that various compounds are produced for energy off of the substrates.

Some common substrates that may be handled in the body include:

- **Carbohydrates.** These are organic compounds that produce the tissues needed for plants and kids to grow.
- **Glucose.** This is a sugar that is found in many animal tissues and fruits. Sometimes the glucose in the body may form through gluconeogenesis.
- **Glycogen.** The compound stores the carbohydrates in animals and human beings.
- **Fat.** This is an organic material that is insoluble in water and is comprised of lipids and proteins. These are used as materials that help structural cells form accordingly, although an excess number of such proteins can be dangerous to a patient.
- **Triglycerides.** These are fatty acids that link up to glycerol compounds and help with storing fats.
- **Protein.** Various amino acids can be consumed and used as protein by the human body. Amino acids help with producing extended polypeptide chains that may help with generating muscle mass.

Functional Biomechanics

There are three aspects of biomechanics that may be noticed regarding the overall functionality of a patient's body:

1. Force

Force produced is a measure of the influence between one object and the next. The force may cause another object to accelerate or decelerate.

2. Torque

Torque is the force that causes rotation to develop. When a load moves closer to where the rotation develops, the torque generated is lower.

3. Lever

A lever is a rigid surface around a stationary weight or fulcrum (the point where an item rests at and where it pivots on.) A first-class lever occurs when the fulcrum is in the middle. For instance, a person who is nodding will notice the fulcrum of the action in the middle. A second-class lever has the resistance being produced in the middle. This occurs as the movement feels more intense midway during the action; the rise of a particular area in the body may be noticed. A third-class lever requires the person to add more physical effort in the middle in order to correctly handle a weight. A curl may produce a third-class lever.

Anatomic Locations

The following is a listing of specific anatomic locations that you may encounter. The positions are organized based on a midline that is produced in the middle part of the body. The midline is vertical and divides the body into left and right halves, similar to a sagittal plane:

- **Superior** – above a certain point
- **Inferior** – below a point
- **Proximal** – near a certain point
- **Distal** – further from that certain point
- **Anterior** – at the front part of the body
- **Posterior** – at the back end of the body
- **Medial** – near the midline
- **Lateral** – away from the midline
- **Contralateral** – on opposite sides of the body
- **Ipsilateral** – on the same side

Principles of Motor Development

Motor development is required for ensuring there are no problems with how the body evolves and grows.

Motor Behavior

Motor behavior refers to the ways the body responds to various stimuli. The motor behavior process consists of:

1. **Motor Control**

Motor control refers to how the CNS handles sensory information through prior events.

2. **Motor Learning**

In motor learning, a person develops certain motor control functions through practice, thus increasing the patient's ability to handle proper skilled motions.

3. **Motor Development**

Motor development refers to how motor skills change over time.

The Use of Feedback in Motor Learning

Feedback is a necessity for motor learning as it concentrates heavily on how sensory data is processed. As the Health Monitoring System (HMS) manages sensory data, it becomes easier for motor learning functions to move forward. The feedback that is produced will focus mainly on points within the body, plus actions that may develop outside of the body and influence its natural functionality.

Internal Feedback

Internal feedback develops as sensory data is used to monitor a person's movements or any changes that might develop in the environment a person is in. The body requires proper analysis and control for ensuring it is capable of managing key physical functions.

External Feedback

External feedback comes from an outside source, such as another person's feedback or some kind of recording. The data may then be used to manage certain actions.

Other Considerations

- **Muscle synergies** – Synergies occur as muscle groups are managed by the CNS to support movements.
- **Proprioception** – The sensory input produced throughout the body from many receptors is called proprioception. Part of this includes managing limb movements while identifying how the body senses a certain position.
- **Sensorimotor integration** – The integration process involves how well the nervous system can take in information and whether a proper motor response is produced based on how well the body handles changes.

Nutritional Considerations

Macronutrients

Macronutrients are significant types of compounds that are required for energy. These are often burned off in workouts and may help with restoring many bodily functions.

Carbohydrates

Carbohydrates are sugars, starches and fiber compounds. These are used by the body for energy.

The basic forms of carbs are:

1. **Monosaccharide**

This is a singular sugar unit, including fructose or glucose. You may find some of these sugar units in natural grains and fruits.

2. **Disaccharide**

This is where two sugar units are featured at a time, such as sucrose, lactose and maltose. These are often slightly harder for the body to break down. Dairy products often include many of these sugar compounds.

3. **Fiber**

A complex carbohydrate, fiber produces bulk in the digestive system and is heavily associated with promoting regularity. Fiber regulates how glucose is processed. Fiber may be found in a soluble or insoluble form. The soluble form is dissolved in water and reduces the patient's blood glucose level and cholesterol level alike. Insoluble fiber form cannot be dissolved in water and may be more difficult for the body to process.

Glucose and Glycogen and their Influence on Blood Sugar (Glycemic Index)

Glucose and glycogen are carbohydrates that heavily impact a person's blood sugar level. Glucose is a monosaccharide which is made in the body through proteins and fats, as well as some carbs. The compound is used as energy for physical activities. Glycogen is a complex carbohydrate that stores energy in the liver and muscle tissue. The two compounds directly influence how a patient's glycemic index (GI) is measured. The GI is a rate at which carbs will raise blood sugar levels, thus influencing the patient's ability to produce insulin. When the patient has a lower GI level, carbohydrates are digested slowly. This keeps blood glucose levels from rising, therefore preventing high levels of insulin production.

The body's GI can be measured as follows:

High = 70 or greater

Moderate= 56 to 69

Low = 55 or lower

Necessary Carbohydrate Consumption

A patient requires four calories for each gram of carbohydrates consumed. This should equal around six to 10 grams per kilogram of weight each day. About 28 to 40 grams of the carbohydrates one consumes should be from fiber. Carbohydrates can make up at least half of a patient's diet, but they can also comprise up to 65 percent of a diet.

Using Carbs for Performance Intentions

A person may consume a meal rich in carbohydrates about two to four hours before a workout. About 1.5 grams of carbs for every kilogram of weight may also be consumed about 30 minutes before a workout to increase the patient's glycogen stores, thus improving upon that person's ability to manage a proper workout. A person who plans on working out for at least 60 minutes will need about 30 to 60 grams of carbs per hour.

Protein

Protein consists of amino acids that are connected through peptide bonds. It is critical for the production of healthy tissues. As a patient exercises and uses up energy, protein is saved in the body and used to repair tissues following a workout. Part of this includes ensuring the tissues that are grown during workouts stay strong. But when the energy balance is at a negative total, the amino acids are broken down and are instead used for energy, thus allowing gluconeogenesis (allowing fats and carbs to be stored while proteins are broken down) to develop.

The Essential Amino Acids

For the body to develop healthy muscles, a patient must consume essential amino acids, either though foods or supplementation; these cannot be manufactured by the human body. The essential amino acids required are:

1. Leucine
2. Lysine
3. Tryptophan
4. Valine

5. Threonine
6. Phenylalanine
7. Histidine
8. Isoleucine
9. Methionine

Nonessential Amino Acids

Nonessential amino acids are produced within the body and do not require further supplementation. Such amino acids are:

1. Alanine
2. Asparagine
3. Serine
4. Glutamic acid
5. Aspartic acid
6. Selenocysteine
7. Pyrrolysine

Complete vs. Incomplete Proteins

Complete proteins provide a person with all the necessary essential amino acids. Incomplete proteins do not contain all of the amino acids, though they may include some.

Necessary Protein Consumption

A patient requires four calories for every gram of protein consumed. A person requires 0.4 grams per pound per day. Strength-training athletes need 0.5 to 0.8 grams per pound per day. Endurance athletes require around 0.5 grams per pound each day. Proteins should make up about 10 to 35 percent of a patient's diet.

Fat

Fats are designed to trigger functions in the human body for energy. Fats help with insulating tissues and securing critical organs, producing proper cellular membranes to encourage correct cellular function and controlling how digestive functions work. Most fats in the body are triglycerides. This is a chemical type of fat that is often found in foods and can be found in the body after the person consumes these.

There are three forms of fat:

1. **Monounsaturated**

A monounsaturated fat is a lipid that is missing a hydrogen atom. This includes a double bond. Foods with monounsaturated fats include olive oils, peanuts and avocados. This is considered to be an unsaturated fatty acid. This may increase HDL cholesterol and should be consumed in moderation.

2. **Polyunsaturated**

A polyunsaturated fat is a lipid with many points of unsaturated fats. Soy and sunflower oils are prominent polyunsaturated fats. Omega-3 fatty acids are also considered in this category.

3. **Saturated**

Saturated fats are found in meats, dairy products and some oils, such as coconut oil. Saturated fats cause an increase in LDL cholesterol. Some of these saturated fats include trans fats that are utilized to allow foods to last longer; these may be more dangerous to the body than basic saturated fats due to the added compounds.

Appropriate Fat Consumption

A patient requires nine calories for every gram of fat consumed. The fats should total around 25 to 35 percent of one's basic consumption each day.

Micronutrients

Micronutrients are vitamins and minerals that a patient requires. These are naturally found in various foods, although a person may also consider supplementation. Some of the most important micronutrients include the following.

1. **Calcium**

Calcium creates stronger teeth and bones but is also needed for improving muscle contractions and how the body metabolizes energy. Calcium can also prevent excess fats from developing by preventing the production of calcitrol, a hormone that prompts fat-storage efforts in the body. A patient requires about 1,000 mg of calcium each day, although that total may go up to 1,200 mg after age 50. Up to 2,000 mg should be used each day to keep the patient's blood stores healthy. Anything extra may cause an excess amount of calcium to persist in the blood, thus making it harder to lose weight. Typical dairy products like milk contain calcium. Those who struggle to consume dairy products due to an allergy or intolerance may consume sesame seeds or sardines, among other oily fish and legumes. Supplementation may be required in cases where a person is not getting enough calcium from his or her diet.

2. **Vitamin D**

Vitamin D helps the body absorb the calcium it takes in. This, in turn, assists in supporting muscle contractions. Around 10 to 20 mcg of vitamin D is needed in an average day. Supplementation with 25 to 100 mcg of vitamin D can also be utilized to keep the vitamin consistent within the patient's bloodstream. Vitamin D can be found in oily fish and eggs.

3. **Iron**

Iron is a micronutrient that moves oxygen from the lungs to the muscles. This helps with managing proper energy levels and can improve upon how the body's immune system operates. For men, 19.3 to 20.5 mg of iron should be utilized each day. The total for women is 17 to 18.9 mg per day. Most types of meats contain added iron deposits.

4. **Vitamin C**

Vitamin C, or ascorbic acid, assists in helping the body to break down carbohydrates for energy. The risk of oxidative stress produced by a workout is reduced by vitamin C consumption, as is the risk of infection. Men should consume 90 mg of vitamin C each day. The total for women is 75 mg. Vitamin C is found mainly in citrus fruits.

5. **Selenium**

Selenium prevents free radicals from impacting the body during a workout. As selenium works, oxygen is secured and moved through the lungs, reducing the potential for oxygen atoms to become free radicals. The nutrient may also improve the body's immune system, thus preventing infections from possibly developing. Fifty-five mcg of selenium is needed each day. For a pregnant woman, the total may increase to 60 mcg.

6. **Copper**

Copper is a trace micronutrient found mainly in nuts. Copper strengthens tendons around the body, thus improving weight-lifting functions. Around two mg of copper may be consumed in a day.

7. **Magnesium**

Magnesium prevents muscle cramping, thus reducing the potential for injuries during a workout. Around 400 mg can be used by men each day. The total needed for women is 300 mg. Magnesium is found in leafy green vegetables and in some nuts and seeds.

Toxicity

Patients should be cautious about how many vitamins they take, to avoid potential overconsumption and toxicity. The symptoms of toxicity are difficult to identify. In most cases, the toxicity entails an excess amount of one nutrient canceling out the effects of another nutrient, thus creating a dramatic imbalance in how the body is being supported by such nutrients. In other cases, excess totals of various nutrients may cause heart irregularities and breathing difficulties.

Hydration

The human body requires regular hydration. As about 60 percent of the body consists of water, it is critical to ensure the body receives the water that it needs. Dehydration has a negative impact on the body's circulatory functions. Furthermore, a patient's athletic performance may be dramatically impacted by dehydration.

Daily Water Consumption Needs

A man should consume three liters of water a day. A woman should take in 2.2 liters of water a day. A patient should also add about eight ounces of water each day for every 25 pounds that a person is deemed to be overweight. The added fluid is to trigger the body's natural metabolic functions, thus potentially improving upon how well the body can burn off excess weight. In cases where a patient exercises for 60 minutes or longer, a sports drink with up to eight percent of its total including carbohydrates may be consumed. This may restore the body's natural functions and provide added energy.

Additional Notes About Water Consumption

Water should be consumed evenly throughout the day to improve upon how active the body is, while also allowing the body's metabolic process to stay consistent. Cold water may help improve upon how metabolic processes work; the added cold temperature requires the body to adjust its metabolic efforts to regulate the body's temperature. Any flavorings or additives should be avoided if possible. Although flavored drinks may work to restore electrolytes during workouts, they may also contain extra sugar. Plain cold water is best for avoiding both dehydration and extra calories.

Units of Energy Measurement

The calorie is the main unit of energy measurement. The calorie is the total amount of heat energy needed to raise a single gram of water by one degree Celsius.

Caloric Intake and Expenditure Needs

Caloric intake refers to how many calories a person consumes in a day. The total is critical to managing one's body and determining how well it can handle a workout plan.

Daily energy expenditure is the number of calories that a person burns for energy in a day. In order to lose weight, a patient needs to burn more calories than he or she consumes. A man requires 2,500 calories per day to maintain his weight and 2,000 calories per day to lose one pound of weight each week. A woman requires 2,000 calories per day for maintenance and 1,500 calories per day in order to lose a pound each week.

Energy Usage

- **Resting Metabolic Rate** – The RMR is a measure of the amount of energy that a person uses while at rest.
- **Thermal Effect of Food** – The TEF is the energy that is used within the body for handling digestive functions. About six to 10 percent of the body's daily expenditure consists of the TEF.
- **Energy in Physical Activity** – The amount of energy used during a physical activity session should be around 20 percent of a person's total expenditure during a typical day.

Dietary Reference Intakes

Dietary references intakes, or DRI, refers to the total of what a person should consume each day. This will vary based on health goals, age, gender, weight and build, among other factors.

Three factors may be used when reviewing the DRI for a patient:

1. **Recommended Dietary Allowance** – The RDA is the average amount of a nutrient that a person must consume each day in order to remain healthy.
2. **Tolerable Upper Intake** – The UL is the highest amount of a nutrient that can be consumed without risk of toxicity.
3. **Adequate Intake** – The AI is a measure of the daily amount of a nutrient required for allowing nutrients to be consumed accordingly.

Portion Sizes, Meal Timing and Frequency

Basic Needs

It's important to review a patient's daily caloric intake to determine whether this is likely to cause weight loss or the inverse. Patients are encouraged to eat foods that are high in fiber and low on the glycemic index. These include whole wheat grains and non-starchy vegetables as well as most fruits.

Fat Loss

A patient needs about four to six small meals each day. Having smaller portions throughout the day improves upon the body's ability to handle hunger and allows blood sugar levels to remain stable throughout the day. It may also help with maintaining energy levels. Fewer than 10 percent of calories should be saturated fats. The proteins, carbs and fats that a patient consumes should also be divided up evenly throughout the day for the best results. Any foods that have been heavily processed may contain a lack of nutrients and therefore should be avoided. Patients who need to consume fewer than 1,200 calories in a day should consult a doctor for further guidance. Such diets might be dangerous to some patients.

Lean Mass Support

Proteins should be divided up evenly throughout the day's meals. Carbs and proteins should be consumed about 90 minutes before exercise, to allow for the body to recover and for proteins to be utilized. Patients should still consume some fats, as they're important for bodily functions, but excess fats are to be avoided.

Crash and Fad Diets

Crash and fad diets are significant modifications that people make to their routines in an attempt to lose weight very rapidly. In most cases, these diets do not entail much physical activity. A patient may also engage in excess workouts, possibly causing some tissues to break down. Also, a patient may experience a decline in the number of healthy nutrients regularly consumed. For instance, a patient might focus on only one particular food or compound within a period of time. In many cases, such diets will last for a few days at a time. This practice may be dangerous as it can deprive the patient of critical nutrients, increasing the risk of ill health and injury.

Nutritional Supplements

Nutritional supplements may help the body absorb certain nutrients. While these may be prescribed to patients, they should not be used in place of a proper diet; some supplements may not be easy for the body to process as the digestive system might break down the components of those nutrients.

Some of the more commonly used nutritional supplements include:

- **Individual micronutrient supplements.** Such supplements provide a person with a high dosage of the proper nutrient that one needs. A supplement has to be analyzed based on its content, and one's daily dietary intake to avoid toxicity.

- **Creatine.** Creatine is often used in supplementation programs to produce phosphate, added muscle mass and strength. The body's anaerobic performance may also improve during the workout process. About 20 grams can be used each day for five to seven days, with two to five grams used each day for maintenance after that.

- **Caffeine.** Naturally found in coffee and other drinks, caffeine can help with improving how the body focuses on a workout routine. About three to six mg for each kilogram of weight may be used about an hour before a workout, although a person should start off slow first, to see how well the body responds. Some people may experience increased heart rates, hypertension and general restlessness.

Anabolic Steroids

Anabolic steroids are often utilized as androgens that are synthetic in build and work with testosterone to build muscle mass. Although people may use these during a workout routine to build muscle mass, the patient risks the development of feminization around parts of the body from testosterone deposits breaking down over time. Some steroids must be injected, thus making it difficult for the body to process the steroids. There is also the risk of infection or inflammation at or around the injection site. Anabolic steroids are illegal for bodybuilding use, as per the World Anti-Doping Agency. Therefore, it is recommended that a person avoids using anabolic steroids.

Food and Supplement Label Reading

Various elements are required on labels according to various national health organizations such as the United States Food and Drug Administration:

1. Serving size

The serving size recommendation will vary by person.

2. Basic components

Each food or supplement will have a series of nutrients; this includes a listing of how many grams or other units of measurement are found in each of these products.

3. Daily value

The daily value is based on an average of 2,000 calories that one may consume in a day. The daily value total may vary based on the person.

4. Added ingredients

The bottom part of a label may include details on any flavors, fillers, binders and other items that have been added to the product. These are additives that will not provide the patient with any substantial benefits or support. Some products may be organic, but there are also some artificially-produced items.

Factors That Influence Weight Management

Law of Thermodynamics

The law of thermodynamics states that energy cannot be created or destroyed when in an isolated system. Therefore, there has to be a balance between calories consumed and calories expended. A person must consume enough calories to provide energy while working out, improving upon how well the body burns off fats. An excess of calories and a lack of physical activity will have the inverse effect.

Sleep

Sleep is necessary for weight management. Patients who sleep seven or fewer hours of sleep a night are at an elevated risk of gaining weight or may struggle to lose weight. A sleep journal can be kept to document how well someone is sleeping, how that person feels after waking up and how well the body is advancing through a workout or fitness routine. The journal may identify some trends that suggest how well a person is finding ways to develop a healthy routine or whether there are concerns that are not working accordingly. A sleep journal may also help a person to develop a consistent sleep schedule, going to be at a certain hour in the evening and then getting up at a specific time in the morning. A consistent sleep schedule is necessary for good health, supporting the full restoration of the body's metabolic processes and allowing for the proper processing of nutrients.

Endocrine Functions

The endocrine system must be monitored regularly to ensure the proper hormones are being produced to help a person manage his or her weight. Malfunctioning glands may influence how well a person's body functions. Some of these concerns include:

1. **Cushing Syndrome**

Cushing syndrome occurs as the body produces excess amounts of cortisol. The added production causes weight gain to develop. While cortisol is necessary for converting fat into energy during a workout, an excess total will keep that compound from working as intended. The excess cortisol will cause the body to gain weight as the body doesn't know what to do with the surplus.

2. **Hypothyroidism**

Hypothyroidism occurs when the thyroid gland is unable to produce enough metabolic hormones. This may cause a person to gain weight and develop joint pains. A person with hypothyroidism may start to feel sluggish and worn out during a workout, thus struggling to get through a workout routine.

3. Diabetes

Diabetes develops as the pancreas is unable to produce insulin accordingly. Regular insulin injections or medications are then required. The disorder may cause a person to develop fatigue during a workout and can cause a person's nerves to become increasingly sensitive and increases the risk of developing damage to things such as the feet and eyes.

4. Addison's Disease

Addison's disease, a very rare condition, occurs as the adrenal glands are attacked by the body. The glands will not produce the natural steroid hormones that the body requires for building mass, and a person may experience intense fatigue. A person will require corticosteroid treatments to control the issue.

Medication

Some medications may influence how well a person can maintain his or her weight. The use of certain medications may be dangerous to some people due to how they can stimulate a person's appetite or cause the body's metabolic rate to lessen. Before prescribing a workout routine, you may consider asking a patient about the medications he or she is taking. Asking questions about such medications may help with identifying any concerns surrounding weight loss efforts or attempts to stay healthy.

Ask about any of these medications; the following may cause a person to gain weight or struggle to produce healthy muscle mass:

- Antidepressants, including sertraline
- Diabetes medications like sulfonylureas
- Beta-blockers and other medications used for reducing blood pressure levels
- Prednisone and other steroidal hormone drugs
- Drugs for controlling epilepsy, such as valproate
- Antipsychotic drugs, including lithium or clozapine

Some medications may also cause a person to lose weight unintentionally. These medications may be dangerous to the body as they cause muscle mass and other tissues to wear out prematurely.

Such medications include:

- Antibacterial medications like metronidazole
- Antifungal medications like amphotericin
- Any medications known to suppress a patient's appetite
- Bronchodilators for the treatment of asthma and other chronic breathing issues; medications that include salbutamol sulphate
- Stimulant drugs like phentermine; while this may help with triggering some weight loss during a healthy diet, the drug may accelerate that weight loss to a potentially dangerous total

You may refer a client to a doctor to identify the problem in further detail. A person should not discontinue the use of any medication without first consulting a physician. In some cases, a doctor might prescribe an alternate medication that has less of an impact on weight loss or gain.

Questions

1. The following segment of the nervous system is responsible for identifying a sensory response:
    a. Sensory
    b. Integrative
    c. Motor
    d. Kinetic

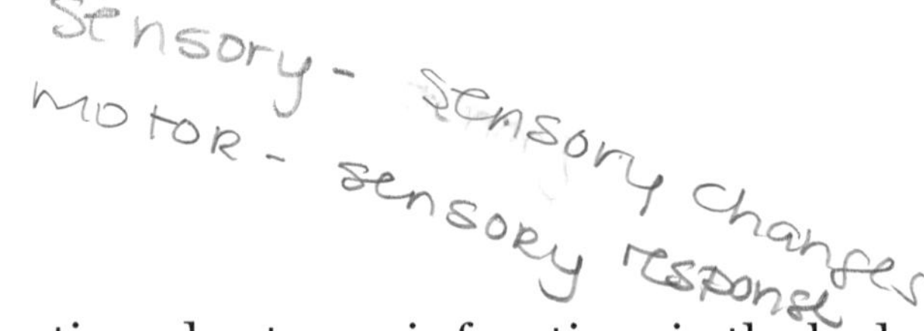

2. The main difference between somatic and autonomic functions in the body entails:
    a. Voluntary concepts
    b. How the heart functions
    c. What is influenced by exercise
    d. How the body restores itself in rest

3. The outermost part of the muscle tissue in the body is the:
    a. Epimysium
    b. Perimysium
    c. Endomysium
    d. Tendon

4. The main point that differentiates the agonist in a muscle movement from the synergist is:
    a. The type of movement functions
    b. The stability of the movements
    c. The amount of power produced
    d. How the body relaxes

5. Epinephrine, or adrenaline, is regularly released by the body as a means of handling:
    a. Fatigue
    b. Sudden twitching movements
    c. Energy
    d. Stress

6. The transverse abdominis muscles assist in keeping the spinal column:
    a. Flexible
    b. Stiff
    c. Capable of rotating
    d. Thick

7. The bone structure is supported through processes and projections that support the bones as they link up to:
   a. Nerves
   b. Muscles
   c. Tendons
   d. Organs

8. The following may protect the body from infections:
   a. White blood cells
   b. Clotting compounds
   c. Lymphatic nodes
   d. Atrium

9. This part of the heart takes in blood through the lungs:
   a. Left atrium
   b. Right atrium
   c. Left ventricle
   d. Right ventricle

10. The following veins in the heart are the smallest:
    a. Capillaries
    b. Venules
    c. Arterioles
    d. Arteries

11. The following gland in the endocrine system is necessary for triggering regular sleep functions:
    Pineal produces melatonin
    a. Pineal
    b. Thyroid
    c. Hypothalamus
    d. Thymus

12. The main difference between the concentric and eccentric motions in the body entails how the muscle is physically laid out. The concentric motion involves the muscle being:
    a. Shortened
    b. Lengthened
    c. Widened
    d. Dilated

13. According to Davis's Law, the process for soft tissue healing entails:
    a. Consistent rest
    b. Regular stretching
    c. Using variable times for periods in between workout sets or sessions
    d. The same process in which the tissues were stressed or damaged

14. The main difference between synovial and non-synovial joints is:
    a. Positioning
    b. Size
    c. Bone structure
    d. Movements

15. Plantarflexion is the process of how the ankle joint functions. In this situation, the ankle will:
    a. Flex its position
    b. Stay straight in its layout
    c. Extend its position
    d. Bend accordingly

16. Lactose is a sugar that includes one or more of the following:
    a. pH level
    b. Fiber
    c. Glycogen
    d. Added sugar units

Lactose is a disacchriade

17. Caffeine may be utilized to provide energy. A person who wants to start using caffeine during workouts should start by using the following amount of caffeine for every kilogram of weight:
    a. 3 mg
    b. 6 mg
    c. 8 mg
    d. 12 mg

18. A person who begins to feel tired during a workout, even after consuming enough carbohydrates and electrolytes, may experience concerns with the following part of the endocrine system:
    a. Thyroid gland
    b. Parathyroid gland
    c. Pancreas
    d. Adrenal gland

19. All of these medications can cause weight gain except for:
    a. Sertraline
    b. Lithium
    c. Prednisone
    d. Phentermine

20. Any patient who takes medications may be referred to a doctor to see if the person should do the following when it comes to managing a workout routine:
    a. Decrease dosage
    b. Stop the use of the drug altogether
    c. Find a replacement
    d. All of the above

Answers

1. c. The sensory segment focuses on identifying sensory changes. The motor segment concentrates on the sensory response and what may develop.
2. a. Somatic functions involve the body responding to functions in a voluntary manner, while autonomic functions involve involuntary actions in the organs that naturally take place on their own.
3. a. The epimysium is a border of sorts that protects the muscle tissue from possible damages.
4. c. While the stabilizer focuses on keeping the tissue stable, and the antagonist allows the area to relax, the agonist focuses on producing the most power in a movement.
5. d. In addition to managing allergic reactions, the compound is naturally released in the body when it is stressed. This may help with providing energy to the body to keep it functional.
6. b. The stiffness in the system is required for keeping signals within the body moving accordingly. This may improve upon how well the body responds to various motions and actions.
7. b. The process features are required for ensuring that muscles can link to bones and these tissues are kept insulated and protected against any possible harm.
8. a. Although clotting compounds are vital for preventing excess bleeding, and the lymphatic nodes are needed for carrying out waste, it is the white blood cells that are responsible for neutralizing any possible infections that may enter the body.
9. a. Blood enters the heart from the lungs through the left atrium. The right atrium takes in blood from the rest of the body.
10. b. Venules are the smallest veins that connect to capillaries. The capillaries, in turn, are smaller than the arterioles, which link to the arteries that move blood away from the heart.

11. a. The pineal gland produces melatonin, to help trigger sleeping functions.
12. a. Concentric motions cause muscles to shorten as the force produced is greater than the resistance force.
13. d. For a muscle to grow, according to Davis's Law, the muscle must restore itself over time. The muscle must therefore not be weakened due to a lack of movement for an extended period of time.
14. d. A synovial joint will be secured through the joint capsule and will produce a high range of motion. A non-synovial joint will not entail any movements that may go through.
15. c. Dorsiflexion causes the ankle to flex in its position while plantarflexion causes the ankle to extend.
16. d. Lactose is a disaccharide, which means that the compound will store multiple amounts of sugar at a time. Two sugar units are included in each compound.
17. a. A person can handle three to six mg of caffeine for every kilogram of weight, but a person should start with a three mg dosage. The key is to confirm that a person is capable of handling the physical impacts that may come with caffeine consumption without experiencing any possible side effects.
18. a. A person who develops consistent sluggishness and fatigue in a workout might be experiencing hypothyroidism. This develops as a person is unable to produce the metabolic hormones that are needed for a healthier routine.
19. d. Phentermine and other stimulants will help with improving how well the body can handle certain weight loss processes, although the added medication may cause some risks relating to the body producing a faster metabolic rate than normal. A patient's response to the medication will vary.
20. d. Each of these solutions may work, although it might be best to try and find an alternative first.

Domain 2: Assessment

The assessment part of your CPT functionality involves reviewing the needs that a patient has and how a workout plan should be adjusted accordingly. The details you come across in the assessment process may help with identifying any medical issues that a person might have which might have an impact on his or her activity level.

PAR-Q Assessment

The Physical Activity Readiness Questionnaire may be filled out to allow a participant to identify his or her ability to exercise. Part of this includes recognizing whether a person is ready to engage in physical activities or if there is a risk associated with the process. Any client who answers "yes" to at least one of the questions involved in the PAR-Q assessment should be referred to a physician for added support.

There are seven questions that must be included in the PAR-Q assessment:

1. Have you been diagnosed with a heart condition that will inhibit your ability to be physically active unless cleared by a doctor?
2. Do you experience chest pains while exercising?
3. Have you developed chest pains in the past month at times when you were not working out or being physically active?
4. Do you ever lose your balance due to dizziness? Have you ever lost consciousness?
5. Do you have joint or bone issues that may become worse due to changes in physical activities?
6. Are you taking any medications for blood pressure or for a heart condition?
7. Do you know of anything else that may make engaging in physical actions dangerous to your healthy?

A proper medical evaluation is required for anyone who answers "yes" to any of these questions. Accordingly, you may refer the person for a follow-up.

Subjective vs. Objective Information

You will have to ask both subjective and objective information of your patients to get an idea of how healthy they are and what their habits are like, both good and bad.

Subjective Information

This refers to basic details on a person's life, including:

- Medical history
- Occupation
- Lifestyle; this includes any hobbies or dietary considerations
- Further personal information

Objective Information

This focuses mainly on the specifics relating to how a patient's body functions. This includes details on:

- Blood pressure
- How well a patient performs on physical tests
- A review of posture
- Cardiorespiratory reviews
- A basic analysis of the body's overall composition

General Activity Considerations

Multiple concerns may be noted regarding a person's history with certain physical actions or routines. Part of this includes a look at:

- **Extended sitting periods.** A person who sits for far too long might develop tightness around the hip flexors. The upper back may also develop a rounded feeling. The head may also move forward too much.
- **Repeated motions.** Pattern overload may develop in some cases. This includes cases where the muscles in a certain part of the body keep on moving in the same direction with no real variation involved.
- **Wearing dress shoes.** For women, high heels can cause the calves to become overly tight. For men, a plantarflexed layout can cause flat feet, a case where the pronation in the feet becomes too intense or is otherwise difficult to work with.
- **Mental and emotional stresses.** The scalenes may start to shorten while the upper trapezius contracts. The patient's heart rate and blood pressure may also increase to potentially unhealthy levels.

Medical Risk Factors

Past health concerns must be identified when reviewing a person's health. These have to be identified when planning a routine, in order to lessen the risk of injury during a workout.

Prior Injuries or Surgical Procedures

A patient who has experienced a substantial injury in the past or has undergone a surgical procedure may be at an elevated risk of developing possible future medical concerns. Injuries to certain joints, particularly the knees and ankles, are often signs of possible damages to neural controls. An ankle sprain may reduce the neural control around the gluteus maximus and medius, for instance. A knee injury can reduce the control around the kneecap and muscles in the surrounding areas.

Core stabilization muscles may also cause low back problems, depending on how well they are laid out and how they can support the patient's body. This can cause substantial issues in how stable the body is, depending on how well the area operates for most physical functions. Shoulder injuries can cause the rotator cuff to wear out prematurely. This can happen as neural controls in the area are substantially impaired, and it becomes harder for the body to manage basic functions.

Chronic Illnesses and Diseases

Chronic illnesses and diseases may have developed multiple times in a year or could have been persistent throughout a patient's life. These include conditions that do not go away and others that occasionally recur. Patients who have experienced hypertension, diabetes, various cancers or other chronic conditions are at an elevated risk of experiencing substantial physical concerns.

Medication Use

A medication may potentially impact a person's ability to exercise or to stay healthy in some form. Not all people who use medications will experience these issues, but patients should still be monitored accordingly.

Some of the more common issues surrounding medication use in a patient include the following:

- Weight gain
- Unplanned weight loss
- Changes in bowel movements; this may include increased urination, diarrhea or constipation

- Changes in blood pressure; some medications may raise it while others lower it
- Weakening of the immune system
- Changes in heart rate

You may need to talk with a patient about the medications he or she is using and about any potential side effects. You can refer a person to a doctor for added help in cases where that person might have significant issues regarding a medication that have to be discussed in further detail.

Chronic Pain

Chronic pain refers to a case where a person experiences an intense amount of pain. This pain may be recurring and persistent in many cases and may not be easily treated.

Some of the more common types of chronic pain that a person may experience include:

1. **Nociceptive Pain**

This form of pain occurs as the soft tissues experience consistent pain. The body's nociceptors or sensory nerves send signals of pain to the spinal column and to the brain. Arthritis and fibromyalgia are among the more common forms of nociceptive pain.

2. **Visceral Pain**

Visceral pain involves nociceptors with organs sending signals out. These pains focus on very specific organs. Endometriosis and cystitis are among the more difficult forms of visceral pain that a person may experience.

3. **Neuropathic Pain**

Neuropathic pain involves the body experiencing sudden pains around the body due to the nerves not functioning accordingly. The nerves may send out the incorrect signals relating to how well the body may respond to illnesses or sudden actions. Sciatica is one form of neuropathic pain. Talk with a patient about the pain he or she has and how frequently that pain is felt. Be sure to discuss any medications being taken for the pain.

Elements of Lifestyle Questionnaire

An elements of lifestyle questionnaire should include a series of questions to analyze a person's basic living functions. Some of the more common questions that may be asked include the following:

Sleep

- What is your wake and sleep cycle like?

- How long does it take for you to get to sleep?
- How rested do you feel after sleeping?
- Does your sleep cycle ever change depending on certain things that happen in your life?

Daily Routine

- Do you rely on caffeine to help yourself stay awake and alert?
- How often do you go outdoors on a typical day?
- How often do you work, and when do you work? What is your profession?
- Do you set any goals for what you do in a typical day?

Personal Events

- Have you gone through any substantial events in your life that have changed your regular routines or behaviors?
- What are your hobbies?

Health

- What efforts have you put into getting the most out of your health?
- Do you smoke or drink? If so, when was the last time you did either? How often do you do either?
- What are your dietary goals?
- How positive are you about your body? Do you have any issues with your body that you would like to try and fix on your own?

Cardiorespiratory Assessments

Cardiorespiratory assessments are necessary for identifying a patient's maximum oxygen uptake of VO2MAX. These may also help with identifying how well the body can move forward in a workout routine. Some of the more common assessments that may be used include:

3-Minute Step Test

The three-minute step test is used to identify a person's heart rate and effort. A person who is closer to a maximum rate will have an easier time with getting the most out of a workout.

1. A patient performs 96 steps on a 12-inch step in a minute. This is repeated for three minutes.
2. The patient's recovery pulse is measured about five seconds after the person stops.
3. The pulse is measured based on how well the pulse is listed versus the three maximum heart-rate zones (MHR) that may be attained in a test. These three zones will be discussed further in this section.

Rockport Walk Test

The Rockport walk test is a measure used to identify the patient's heart rate:

1. Record the patient's weight at the start.
2. About five to ten minutes of light stretching is recommended before the test begins.
3. Have the patient walk for a mile on a treadmill. The treadmill should be at an even level with no incline or decline involved.
4. Record the time that it takes for a person to walk a mile.
5. Take the person's heart rate after the test is completed.
6. The measurements are then measured based on a certain formula:

132.853 – (0.0769 x weight) – (0.3877 x age) – (6.315 x gender) – (3.2649 x time) – (0.12565 x heart rate)

For gender, the variable should be one for men or zero for women. That is, the 6.315 total is only applicable to men. The total produced in the test is a measure of the patient's VO2MAX. The pulse may also be measured and placed in one of three groups, based on the result.

VO2MAX

The VO2MAX is a measure of a patient's maximum oxygen uptake. It is the highest amount of oxygen a person can take in during an intense exercise period. This is a basic measure of endurance. To measure the VO2MAX, a patient needs to wear a breathing mask during a test. This may work during the Rockport walk test or the three-minute step test, although this could also be used on a treadmill that moves at an increasing speed. The VO2MAX may be identified when the patient's oxygen consumption gets to its most intense and it becomes difficult for the body to take in anymore oxygen at that juncture.

A patient's nominal VO2MAX should be at around 30 to 60 mL/min/kg (milliliters of oxygen per minute for each kilogram of weight). The VO2MAX may be monitored on a GPS watch or other fitness tracker. However, a lab test is best as this is more accurate than any device. The VO2MAX has to be measured in a consistently controlled and ventilated environment. Any measurements used by a fitness tracker are intended to be rough estimates. All cardiovascular assessments may be conducted based on a patient's comfort level. You may consider starting a person off at a lower rate of effort to ensure that he or she can handle the work involved. This will help you identify what a person can and cannot do based on current health, level of fitness and prior medical conditions.

Physiological Assessments

Maximum Heart Rate

The MHR is measured as a basic guide for how well a person's heart might beat while physically active. This does not mean that a person is going to attain that MHR. Rather, it is a benchmark that can be used when identifying how well a person can handle certain physical activities.

The MHR may be identified by using the following measurement:

208 – (0.7 x age)

This is an accurate measurement of the MHR a patient may have. A 50-year-old person may have an MHR of 173 beats per minute (208 – (0.7 x 50)). A simplified measurement of 220 minus the patient age may also work to get a baseline estimate, although this total may not be as accurate. For a 50-year-old, the measurement in this instance would be 170 bpm.

General Zones

A patient's results in a cardiorespiratory assessment can be identified in one of three zones. These zones refer to the best possible MHR a patient may achieve:

Zone 1: Fair or poor. This is where a patient's heart rate is 65 to 75 percent of the maximum rate following a test.

Zone 2: Average. The total is 76 to 85 percent of the maximum rate.

Zone 3: Good. The patient's heart rate is 86 to 90 percent of the maximum at this juncture.

For a 50-year-old, a person with a final heart rate of 150 bpm will be in Zone 3. The 150-bpm total is around 88 percent of that person's maximum rate.

Pulse Review

The patient's pulse should be reviewed to get an idea of how well the heart is functioning and how well blood is moving through the patient's body. A radial pulse measurement may be conducted by placing two fingers below the patient's wrist while on the thumb side of the patient's arm. A carotid pulse measurement may be conducted by measuring the pulse on the patient's neck. This is not as effective as a radial pulse, although the patient may be taught how to use the carotid pulse measurement for his or her own personal use.

Resting Heart Rate

The patient's resting heart rate (RHR) is a measure of heart rate when the person is not active. For the best results, this may be taken in the morning. A patient's resting pulse should be tested a few times in a week. This includes working with about three to five straight mornings of test results. The readings can be measured and then averaged out to get an idea of that person's RHR. An average adult should have an RHR between 70 and 80 bpm. The total may be slightly higher for women. The rate should be adhered to in order to avoid any injuries or overexertion during a workout. A patient's RHR should be healthy enough to where that person is not likely to struggle with managing regular physical activities.

Blood Pressure

Blood pressure is a measure of the force of blood on the artery walls. The pressure level has to be optimal to ensure blood can move through the body with the artery walls not experiencing an undue amount of stress. Blood pressure is measured through a standard cuff band that is placed on the upper part of the patient's arm. This adds pressure to the area to get a proper blood pressure readout. Alternatively, a smaller unit may also be placed on the patient's finger in cases where the person might not be ready to handle the pressure of a traditional test.

The test will entail a review of two points:

1. **Systolic.** The systolic pressure refers to the pressure in the arteries after the heart contracts.
2. **Diastolic.** The diastolic pressure is the pressure in the arteries as the heart rests and fills with blood.

A normal blood pressure level will entail a systolic pressure under 120 mmHg and a diastolic pressure under 80 mmHg. A patient with a measurement of 130/80 or higher may be diagnosed as having hypertension or high blood pressure. The intensity of the hypertension will be greater if the patient's numbers are much higher.

Kinetic Chain Checkpoints During Static Posture Assessment

The kinetic chain checkpoints are vital joint areas around the body. These joints must be assessed to identify how well they are aligned throughout the body and that they are active. These areas must be analyzed on the front or anterior, lateral or side, and posterior or rear positions. This is to identify how well the body will stay functional and active.

Ankles and Feet

The ankles and feet should be straight and parallel with each other. The surfaces should be slightly rounded and not flattened. The legs should be propped up at a right angle against the ankles and feet. The heels must also be straight; no pronation should be visible at this point. The gastrocnemius muscle may develop improper shorts in some cases. This may cause the anterior tibalis to become longer than necessary. The peroneals around this area may also become shortened in some of the most improper cases. This includes cases where excess pronation may be found. The condition may be noticed by the gluteus maximus being lengthened.

Knees

The knees must be properly in line with the feet. The feet should be positioned well against the knees without any noticeable pronation. The knees must also avoid being flexed naturally; these areas have to be straight up without being weak or worn.

Lumbo-Pelvic-Hip Complex

The lumbo-pelvic-hip complex (LPHC) has to be level to the floor at a parallel position. Any irregularities where the LPHC tilts back or forth or to the side may be a sign of weakness in the muscles around the general region. The hip flexor complex must be analyzed to see that the muscle is not shortened or being stretched by far too much. The gluteus medius may be analyzed at this point; that muscle may be lengthened if pronation is noticeable.

Shoulders

The shoulders should be level and at an even position that is parallel to the floor. The shoulders should also be positioned normally and should not be rounded or elevated. The latissimus dorsi may also be noticed in this case. The muscle should not be shortened. The transverse abdominis may be lengthened by an excessive total in some of the more intense cases that a patient may experience.

Head and Neck

The head and neck must be measured according to where the areas are neutral and not tilting in an inappropriate manner. The head should not tilt or rotate in any position versus the rest of the neck. The head should not be moving forward from the rest of the body either. A lateral view of the area will provide the best possible vantage point for how well this part of the body is functioning and how easy it is to notice.

Cholesterol

Cholesterol is a fatty compound that is vital for supporting the body's defenses and for producing proper cellular compounds throughout the body. Excess totals of cholesterol may be dangerous for some patients.

A patient's cholesterol may be measured in two forms:

1. **HDL.** High-density lipoprotein cholesterol helps to protect the heart tissue.
2. **LDL.** Low-density lipoprotein cholesterol builds up along the body's arteries and can cause a person's risk of heart disease to increase dramatically.

A patient's cholesterol level should be at 200 mg/dL with the HDL total at greater than 60 and the LDL total under 130. A patient with high cholesterol levels may have a total of 240 mg/dL or greater. The HDL total may be under 40 while the LDL value is greater than 160. The cholesterol total must be measured in a laboratory via a blood sample.

Glucose

The glucose level is a measure of the blood sugar in the patient's body. This is an analysis of how much energy the body has. But the glucose total may also be an analysis of whether a patient has excess sugars in his or her body. This could be a measure of how blood sugar changes over time; those who have higher than average totals of glucose may be at an elevated risk of developing diabetes. A patient's glucose levels may be tested by taking a blood sample after a fasting period. A patient may then be asked to consume a high-glucose compound and then have the blood tested a second time to identify how well the blood sugar levels adjust.

A patient's glucose level while fasting should be at 80 to 100 mg/dL. A patient with a glucose level consistently at 126 or higher may be diagnosed as having diabetes. The glucose level may increase after eating. For a normal body, that total may go to 120 to 140 for about two to three hours after eating. The total may be even higher even before then. A patient whose total is at 200 or greater can be diagnosed with diabetes.

Applicability of Assessment from Other Health Professionals

There may be cases where a physical assessment needs to be fleshed out in further detail, such as with support from another health professional.

Blood Pressure

It is best to have a patient tested for further blood-related issues if a person is deemed to have hypertension. A primary physician may be contacted for help.

Cholesterol

A patient with elevated cholesterol levels should receive proper testing from another professional. This is especially true for cases where the total cholesterol level is 240 mg/dL or higher. Again, it is best to consult a primary physician in this case.

Glucose

A patient should be referred to a doctor if he or she is experiencing very high glucose levels. These include levels of 7.1 mmol/L or higher.

Body Composition Assessments

A patient's body composition can be identified to review whether or not a patient is overweight. Part of this includes an analysis of how well a person's body is laid out and if that person is capable of managing normal exercises or other motions. A person who is overweight is identified as having a body mass index or BMI of 25 to 29.9. A person who is at least 25 pounds over the recommended weight for that person's height may also be identified as being overweight. A person can be identified as being obese if his or her BMI is 30 or greater.

Skinfold

A skinfold test, done on the patient's right side, includes a review of how well the tissues might fold over others. A patient stands up straight while the body is fully relaxed. The skinfolds that are found are measured through a series of calibers. The values of those folds are measured in millimeters, based on how large they are. The totals that are measured will be reviewed and identified to review a patient's total body composition.

Four particular measurements may be used in this case:

1. Biceps via vertical fold test

2. Triceps with another vertical fold test

3. Subscapular through a 45-degree fold test
4. Iliac crest with another 45-degree fold

Again, each of these tests is to be completed along the right side of the patient's body.

The Durnin and Womersley formula may be utilized to get an accurate measurement of the patient's test result. The formula is used to obtain a measurement of the patient's fat percentage. The formula will have to be calibrated based on the patient's age and gender. This may be followed with a basis analysis of how well that person's body is laid out and how well that individual's fat total may be measured. A proper analysis is required in this situation to get a clear idea of what a person's body totals are. Fat mass and lean body mass may both be measured around this point, if needed.

Circumference

Circumference is an analysis of a person's body based on girth. A circumference measurement works with a flexible fabric tape measure:

1. A tape measure is placed around the patient's midsection. The patient should relax and avoid trying to suck anything in.
2. The patient's midsection is measured with the tape. The measuring unit is moved from one end to the next. You are measuring the circumference of the person's body.
3. The result is then reviewed based on the number of centimeters of the circumference.

A man is at an increased risk of physical harm if he has a circumference of 102 cm or greater. A woman will have a higher risk of harm if her circumference is 88 cm or higher. The process may help with identifying the patient's risk of health-related issues and to figure out how much pressure is being added onto the patient's organs, although it is best for an added skinfold test to be used at this point if possible. The circumference test is designed as a general review.

Bioelectrical Impedance

Another practice that may be utilized, bioelectric impedance provides an estimate of the body's composition with an emphasis on body-fat measurements.

The test includes:

1. Two electrodes are placed on the patient's body. One goes on the right hand while the other is on the right foot.

2. An electrical current moves through the body. The current is very light and should not be noticeable by the patient.
3. The bioelectrical impedance machine analyzes the process of fluids and electrolytes moving through the body.
4. The measurement reviews how well the current moves along. While fluids and electrolytes help to carry the signal, fat deposits will cause the signal to slow down.
5. A review of total body water is measured in this process. The analysis then uses an equation to figure out the body fat total.

A machine is used to figure out the proper calculations. This is a helpful process that may be more detailed than a traditional weigh-in, although a person's water level may vary based on any fluids recently consumed.

Performance Assessments

1-Repetition Maximum

The 1-repetition maximum, or RM total, is a measure of the largest amount of weight that a person can lift during a weight-training program. This can be interpreted as a personal record for what someone can lift at a time. This is used to identify what someone can safely work with when lifting weights, although the measurement can also help with getting a person to set a goal for what one can get out of the lifting process in general. The testing process involves stressing a muscle to its highest total. You must perform this test carefully, without risking the patient's health.

The test works as follows:

1. Provide a person with at least 24 hours of rest time before the test.
2. A few warm-up sets should be performed at the start. These are movements that are lighter in weight and will help stimulate the muscles so a more accurate readout can be produced.
3. An appropriate weight is added to a lifting mechanism.
4. The person will demonstrate his or her general ability to handle the weight without issue. This includes being able to complete a full repetition with that weight, although multiple reps may be recommended to confirm a person's ability.

5. The weight that the person can handle is the RM. This is a benchmark for what a person can potentially lift and can be used to guide future lifting exercises.

The process works well for identifying the possible weight a person can handle, but a spotter must always be used to ensure a person is well monitored. Also, the RM measurement can be performed on one of various lifting items. This may work with free weights, although a stationary machine may be best thanks to the safety mechanisms used on such machines to minimize the risk of injury. The practice is ideal for use among most people who wish to lift weights, although this may be dangerous for pregnant women or those who have hypertension or osteoporosis.

Vertical Jump

A vertical jump measurement is an analysis of one's ability to jump high. It measures how high a person can jump while standing still.

The measurement works as follows:

1. A person stands on a flat and even surface.

2. A person's standing reach is measured. This is a measure of how high the hand is from the ground when the hand is raised up all the way.

3. The participant jumps up, with the leg muscles propelling the motion. The person touches his or her hand to a surface to analyze how high up the hand can get.

4. The difference in height between where the standing reach is and where the jumping reach is located is the measurement of how high the reach is.

A man should have a vertical jump of 16 to 19 inches; any jumps of 20 inches or greater may be above average. A woman's vertical jump should be from 12 to 15 inches in high. This total can be over 16 inches for women who are above average. The purpose of the test is to identify the patient's power output. A person who can perform a higher vertical jump will have more energy in the body and will be able to generate the most power by moving the muscles quicker and further. The test works well for people of all heights, although the effort is not suitable for pregnant women.

Long (Broad) Jump

A long or broad jump involves how long a person can jump on a surface. The process requires a person to stand in one place and to then move forward. The jump test measures how powerful the person's legs are, along with how well the person can propel him or herself forward.

1. A person stands at a certain position, on a flat surface.

2. The knees are bent slightly, while the arms are moved back. The head is positioned forward.

3. The person propels him or herself forward as far as possible, staying in a straight line.

4. The distance of the jump is measured based on how far the person lands from the original launch site.

A man should perform a jump about 90 inches in length or greater. A woman's jump should be around 70 inches or longer. The test is effective in reviewing a person's overall sense of power.

Davies Test

The Davies test is a measurement of a person's upper body agility. This includes a review of how well a person can keep his or her body stable in a workout.

1. Place two pieces of tape on the floor, 36 inches apart from each other.

2. Have the person get into a push-up position, one hand touching each piece of tape. This may be a slightly greater distance than what a person is used to in a traditional push-up.

3. The person touches the right hand to the left hand as quickly as possible.

4. The person then touches the left hand to the right hand. Again, this is to be done fast.

5. The person repeats the cycle as many times as possible in 15 seconds.

6. The test is conducted three times, and the results are averaged out.

7. The score is divided by 15 to get a measurement of how many times a movement is made per second.

The test reviews upper body agility. A person with a higher score will have a better agility total and may be capable of handling upper body movements faster than others. The test should not be conducted on those who have had shoulder injuries in the past.

Shark Skill Test

The shark skill test focuses on lower body agility, with an emphasis on analyzing a person's neuromuscular control.

1. Create a 3 x 3 grid on the floor. This should look like a tic-tac-toe grid and should have boxes wide enough to fit a person's feet.

2. A person should stand in the middle box.
3. The person's arms should be positioned on the hips while the left knee is moved upward, with the left foot off of the ground.
4. The person hops from the middle box to other boxes, in a clockwise pattern. The person hops on that right foot to the top center box and then back to the middle, then to the top-right box and then to the middle, and so forth.
5. The test can be repeated with the left foot on the foot, and the right knee bent, while the right foot moves off of the ground.

The test should be reviewed based on three factors:

- How well the person can maintain a sense of balance
- How well that person can stay within the boxes; this is a sign of general control
- How long it takes for a person to go through the entire exercise

Push-Up Test

The push-up test measures a person's upper-body endurance level. The test involves a person being asked to perform as many push-ups as possible in a 60-second period. The optimal result of the push-up test will vary based on a person's gender and age. A man in his thirties should complete 28 to 30 push-ups on average. Meanwhile, he would have to complete 19 to 21 push-ups in his 50s. A woman in her thirties needs 19 to 21 push-ups to be average or 11 to 13 while in her 50s. The test reviews how well a person's upper body can handle repeated motions and manage his or own weight. The test should be handled with caution among those who have experienced shoulder injuries, although this is not as risky as a Davies test.

LEFT Test

The lower extremity functional test reviews a person's agility and ability to accelerate and decelerate.

1. Place two cones about 10 yards from each other.
2. The person sprints from one cone to the next.
3. The person then backpedals to the first cone.
4. That person moves to the side while going from the first cone to the second. This demonstrated how well the body can move sideways and not while sprinting.

The test reviews a person's general sense of agility.

Types of Movement Assessments

Overhead Squat

The overhead squat is a measurement of how well a person's kinetic chain works. The test can be reviewed on all sides of the patient's body to identify how well that person can bend down and move back up while maintaining correct posture. The test may help to identify cases where a person might struggle with some movements or actions when trying to bend down.

1. The test must be performed barefoot. This is to keep a raised heel from possibly influencing the test result.
2. The client's hands are kept straight up.
3. The person squats down as low as possible.
4. The process is repeated about 15 times.
5. Review the person's movement from the anterior, lateral and posterior positions. You can ask to take a video of the person's movement; this should only be done at the participant's discretion.
6. Analyze the anterior position to see if the feet and knees are pointing out in a straight position. A person may have kinetic difficulty if the knees or feet are moving in the wrong directions or are not straight out.
7. Review the lateral position to see if the lower back is arching or rounding. See if the arms are falling forward or if the person is leaning forward far too much.
8. Analyze the posterior view to see if the feet are moving properly or if they are flattening. Look at how the heels are positioned as well; the heels must rise off of the floor. Also, any cases where the weight is shifting off of a base may be a sign of concern.

The measurement will help you to figure out how well a person's form is laid out while exercising. You can use this to educate a person by planning a routine that emphasizes correct positioning.

Single-Leg Squat

The single-leg squat is a measure of how well a person can bend down with one leg. This works with a traditional squat motion.

1. Have the patient bend down with one knee moving forward while the other leg is positioned backward. Make sure the person's back is straight and that the motion is performed without slanting.
2. Review the hip adduction. The patient should not have any adduction.
3. See how the hip is moving based on its basic position. Watch for any case of corkscrewing where the hip appears to be protruding outward.
4. Identify how well a person can maintain his or her balance. That person might be struggling with posture if certain parts of the body have to be favored. This includes cases where an asymmetrical position is necessary in order to stay stable.

The knees may move inward in some cases; this may be a sign that the gluteus muscles are not as active as they are supposed to be. This concern may cause the person to use excess compensation to try and keep his or her body active during a workout.

Gait

A person's gait may be tested to identify how well that person can handle certain physical motions. The test may be completed on a treadmill for the best results.

1. Have a person run on a treadmill at a gentle speed while on a flat slope.
2. Some electrodes may be used around the muscles on the legs. You can link these to a machine to identify muscular signals to see if certain muscles are being favored over others. This may be a sign of a person using some form of muscular compensation.
3. Review the person's motions to see if the feet are pronating or if the leg muscles are shifting in an uneven position. This may include the legs sticking outward or moving inward during some running motions.

Several concerns may be noticed in a gait test:

- The feet are turning outward.
- The knees are pointing inward.
- The LPHC area is rotating too much.
- The shoulders appear to be rounded and not even with the rest of the body.
- The head is tilting forward by too much.

The test can help with starting a plan for managing proper movements and posture or movement correction.

Pulling Functions

A basic pulling test may be utilized to identify how well a person can pull standard weights. This may include working with a lever or pulley that requires extensive effort. The pulling motions may be identified through a variety of workouts. These include arm curls and lifts among other items that require a person to pull a series of weights up and down. The pulling motion should be examined carefully based on a lateral view.

A lateral view is needed to analyze how well the body functions. The following reviews should be completed:

1. The LPHC should be analyzed to see how the lower back acts. The lower back area may start to arch during the lifting process.
2. The shoulder complex should be examined based on how well the shoulders are elevated. In some cases, a person who lifts improperly will lift the shoulders up far too high.
3. The head should be in line with the rest of the body. An improper motion will show that the head is protruding.

Pushing Functions

A pushing test may also be performed. This may include some pressing motions on a stationary lifting unit, with the person standing while performing the movement. A lateral view is needed for reviewing how the person is pushing items. In this case, there are two points to note:

1. The LPHC should be straight with the lower back not arching. Any arching is a sign of the hip flexors being too active.
2. The shoulders should be even and not elevated from the rest of the body. A slight elevation may be a sign of the upper parts of the trapezius being too active.
3. The head should be aligned with the rest of the body and should not be protruding forward during the pushing process.

Body Composition Calculations

Fat Mass

The fat mass is a measure of the patient's body-fat percentage multiplied by the patient's scale weight. The fat percentage should have been gathered through a skinfold measurement. The bioelectrical impedance test can also be used if needed.

Lean Mass

Lean body mass is a measure of the patient's scale weight minus the fat mass that was calculated. The measurement may distinguish cases where a person who is at a higher weight is heavier due to healthy muscle tissues and not from unhealthy fat deposits.

Waist-to-Hip Ratio

The waist-to-hip ratio is a measure of the waist circumference divided by the hip measurement. The measurement process can only be properly carried out if the basic circumference measurements listed earlier have been made correctly. A woman should have a ratio under 0.80. For men, that total should be under 0.95. Any patient who has a ratio greater than those totals will be at a higher risk of diseases relating to being overweight.

BMI Concerns

The body mass index, as measured earlier, can help with identifying if a person is at an elevated risk of developing diseases due to excess weight. A patient with a BMI of 25 or greater is deemed overweight and can be at a higher risk of dealing with certain physical problems. However, the patient's BMI is not intended to be a measurement of a person's body fat. The BMI may be misleading in cases where a person has a good amount of lean muscle mass. The mass may add weight, but it is not necessarily an unhealthy type of weight. Therefore, a proper review of the patient's fat mass and lean mass should be conducted during the measurement process to ensure the patient is healthy.

Considerations for Assessing Specific Persons

Youth

Those who are younger in age should be monitored based on physical features and how well that person is developing. Talk with a youth participant's parents for added information on health and any additional concerns. Strength-based assessments are not necessarily required.

Seniors

Seniors should not be subjected to extensive strength tests. Flexibility tests are not required. Cardio reviews may be performed, although you should avoid anything overtly rough. Seniors don't require body-fold tests in most cases, although basic blood pressure tests are strongly encouraged. Make sure you ask any seniors about medications they may be taken. Such medications may influence how the body will respond to a workout routine.

Obese Patients

A Rockport walk test is encouraged when planning a cardiovascular assessment. A push-up test can be conducted, although a bench or other support feature may be required for supporting the person.

Pregnant Patients

Power and speed-based tests should be avoided. A single-leg balance exercise may be utilized in lieu of a single-leg squat. Overhead squat tests may be performed, although the range of motion involved in the test proccss should be reduced.

Signs a Client Requires a Referral

You will have to refer a client elsewhere in the following cases:

1. A person is suspected of having a medical condition.

You are not allowed to legally diagnose a person with a medical condition unless you have the proper certification for doing so. Refer that person to an outside medical professional.

2. Treatments for certain diseases or injuries are needed.

Your work as a CPT is designed to help people with staying in shape, not to heal diseases or injuries. You must refer a person to a specialist for the treatment of such conditions, especially if they are issues that require extensive monitoring or maintenance.

3. A patient needs to consume a certain diet.

If there are dietary concerns, refer a person to a dietician to help analyze how well that person can handle a workout.

4. A person needs mental health counseling.

You can also refer a person a mental health counselor if you notice that a person is dealing with mental issues that go beyond simply managing time and effort to get physically fit.

Criteria for Reassessment

You may reassess a person to identify whether or not changes should take place within the workout routine. The following four criteria may be used when reassessing a person:

1. Enough time has passed.

You can check on a person's progress every four weeks. You can also review a person sooner if he or she is experiencing any changes in a workout routine.

2. The efforts the person puts in are improving.

You may consider reviewing the patient's needs if that someone's ability to perform certain exercises is visibly improving.

3. The participant wants to adjust his or her goals.

Changes in goals can entail anything from wanting to move towards supporting certain muscle groups to a general design to lose weight in a certain part of the body. You can plan changes in a person's workout routine based on any new goals a person informs you of. This may be helpful, provided that person is realistic about the goals.

4. Sudden lifestyle changes have taken place.

A person may require help if that someone has experienced significant changes in his or her lifestyle. These include changes in diet, any daily routines and cases where a person is no longer smoking or drinking alcohol. Talk with the participant in the program about any changes you can offer to support him or her throughout this situation.

Questions

1. A person who says "yes" to this many questions on the PAR-Q assessment should be referred to a doctor:
    a. 1
    b. 2
    c. 3
    d. 4

2. Objective information regarding a person entails:
    a. Medical history
    b. Posture observation
    c. Lifestyle analysis
    d. Occupational data

3. A three-minute step test requires a person to complete 96 steps on a step that is this high:
    a. 8 inches
    b. 12 inches
    c. 18 inches
    d. 24 inches

4. The Rockport walk test requires a person to complete the following type of walk:
    a. A one-mile job on an oval walking path
    b. A one-mile sprint on a treadmill
    c. A five-minute treadmill run; this may be as long as needed
    d. A one-mile walk on a treadmill

5. A person is experiencing pain, particularly in the liver and kidneys. The following assessment may be conducted:
    a. Skinfold
    b. Circumference
    c. Bioelectrical impedance
    d. BMI measurement

6. A 1-repetition maximum may be performed to identify how much weight a person can handle at a time. The test may work well among:
    a. Pregnant women
    b. Seniors
    c. People with hypertension
    d. People with osteoporosis

7. The long-jump exercise must be planned on the following surface:
   a. A soft space
   b. Sandy materials (i.e., track and field space)
   c. At least 50 feet before the jump point
   d. A flat slope

a flat or hard surface

8. A person who has experienced a shoulder injury in the past should avoid:
   a. Shark skill test
   b. Push-up test
   c. Davies test
   d. LEFT test

9. A patient's body-fat percentage is multiplied by his or her weight. After that, the total is subtracted from the weight. This produces the person's:
   a. Lean mass
   b. Fat mass
   c. BMI
   d. Weight-loss goal

10. Does a younger person require a strength-based test?
   a. Always
   b. Only for those who are larger in size
   c. Only for people who are at risk of obesity
   d. Never

11. A person is experiencing intense mental stress from many outside events. These are causing a person to make different decisions than what he or she would usually make. In this case, you should:
   a. Refer that person to a psychologist
   b. Analyze the patient's issues
   c. Recommend medication
   d. Change the routine

12. For the best workout results, a person's MHR should attain the following percentage; this refers to how close to the MHR a person is after working out:
   a. 65 percent
   b. 75 percent
   c. 85 percent
   d. 90 percent

13. The regression formula for measuring one's MHR is recommended due to the measure being:
    a. More detailed
    b. Accurate
    c. Focused on a person's age
    d. Based on workout routines

14. Any person with hypertension should be monitored based on:
    a. How well a person can pull or push items in a test
    b. A person's ability to recover after a workout
    c. How long it takes to start a workout
    d. Fatigue during a workout

15. The following area around the shoulders may be influenced the most during a workout if the shoulders have experienced an injury in the past:
    a. Scapula
    b. Clavicle
    c. Nerves
    d. Rotator cuff

16. Medications for the following should be examined in the PAR-Q assessment:
    a. Hypertension
    b. Gastric discomfort
    c. Diarrhea
    d. Weakened immune system

17. Anyone who has smoked or consumed alcohol in the past may be consulted in an assessment based on:
    a. How much was smoked or drunk
    b. The last time one smokes or drank
    c. Any routines
    d. All of the above

18. A person who weighs 60 kg should have a VO2MAX of:
    a. 1200
    b. 1500
    c. 1800
    d. 2500

60kg x 30 mL/min

19. When conducting a pulse test, you should review the pulse at this point on the arm:

a. Thumb area
b. Palm
c. Middle part of the forearm
d. Around the joint

20. The resting heart rate may be measured over the course of:
a. 3 to 5 hours
b. 24 hours
c. 3 to 5 days
d. A month

Answers

1. a. The questions are very significant in nature and may directly influence a person's ability to complete certain physical functions.
2. b. The objective information gathered on a person refers to the specific activities he or she may partake in.
3. b. A 12-inch step makes it easier for a person to get up and stay active.
4. d. The one-mile walk provides the participant with a surface for moving so the heart rate and the person's time for getting to the one-mile mark can be measured. The walk should be on an even slope.
5. b. A circumference measurement is needed to identify the possible amount of fat tissue or pressure that is being imposed on the body's midsection. The test reviews the likelihood for organs to experience excess physical pressure and possible harm.
6. b. The other three choices are cases where the testing process may be too risky for a person to participate in. A senior may have an easier time with handling the test, although this is best for cases where a person is prepared to handle the lifting required in the process.
7. d. The long jump must be completed on a flat and hard surface, preferably in an indoor environment without any sand or other cushioning. The exercise does not entail a person getting a running start like what is found in track and field events.
8. c. While a push-up test requires more muscles beyond the shoulder and involves less agility, the Davies test requires fast movements from the shoulder tissues and could be risky to those who have had shoulder injuries in the past.
9. a. The lean mass is a measure of the body's weight subtracted from fat mass.
10. d. A strength test is needed for youth participants.
11. a. A CPT should not try to diagnose mental-health-related issues.
12. d. A person with a higher measure of heart rate versus the maximum will respond well to a workout routine.

13. b. Any MHR measurement is based on age. The reflective measurement is a more accurate choice for measuring the total.
14. b. A person with hypertension may struggle to recover after a workout is completed.
15. d. The rotator cuff will experience tensions and neural dysfunction after an injury.
16. a. If a person is taking blood or heart-rated medications, he or she requires further examination from a doctor.
17. d. Smoking and alcohol habits should be analyzed based on a person's efforts to consistently workout.
18. c. The VO2MAX should be at least 30 mL/min for each kilogram of body weight.
19. a. The thumb area is best, as it is easier for you to find a more accurate readout of the pulse at this point.
20. c. About three to five days of measurements should be performed, with the daily RHR totals being averaged out.

Domain 3: Program Design

An appropriate program must be designed cautiously for the patient's benefit. This is to ensure the patient will feel in control of his or her workout and overall fitness goals.

The SOAP Design Plan

The SOAP plan is used for designing a program that is most efficient and suitable for a person's workout needs. The plan is named for the four parts that are to be utilized.

1. Subjective

A subjective analysis includes a review of a person's body and health. The PAR-Q, or other analytical features, may be utilized. The key is to identify physical history, any lifestyle or occupational concerns, medical issues and any dietary or health concerns that might influence a workout routine.

2. Objective

Objective reviews involve quantified data that may be directly noticed. This includes:

- A person's weight and height
- Blood pressure levels and other vital signs
- Body composition and measurements
- Range of motion
- Endurance testing for the upper and lower body
- A review of a person's posture when standing without outside influences

3. Assessment

An assessment must be made to determine a person's health and personal concerns. The goal here is to help a person determine what she or she needs in a workout or fitness program.

4. Plan

A plan is the summation of points one through three, put into comprehensive action.

Planning a Needs Analysis

A needs analysis may also be utilized in the SOAP process to review any deficiencies a person has, any movements her or she struggles with and any injury sites that need to be strengthened or improved upon.

Main Concepts for Training

Various concepts may be utilized when training the body, such as:

1. The use of body weight

Body-weight training may be considered with exercises that require no added load outside of the body itself. This may be used with all planes of motion in mind.

2. Suspension materials

Anything that may be used to suspend or restrain the body may be used to add pressure and to increase the effort required for certain movements. This may be noticed in resistance training.

3. Free-weight usage

Barbells, kettlebells, medicine balls and any other free weight may be utilized in some actions. The practice will work with all ranges of motion. However, the body must remain stable for those exercises to be completed correctly.

4. Strength-training functions

Some of the more common exercises people can do involve strength-training activities. These are routines where a person focuses on triggering actions in certain muscles. The actions help to both grow muscle mass and to trigger connections between the muscles and the nervous system. These exercises require equipment with immense amounts of weight and a stable layout. Also, the range of motion for such exercises will be heavily limited based on the material being used with the lifting process.

5. Proprioceptive actions

Proprioceptive functions refer to how well a person may work in unstable conditions. Part of this includes cases where the body naturally loses its stability or when a person engages in activities while on an unstable surface. Such actions can trigger new connections between muscles and the nervous system, but they may also be risky if the participant is not prepared to handle certain functions or movements.

Three Basic Stages

Three stages of working out are to be used in the process of planning a workout routine:

1. Stabilization

This is to allow the body to get used to the movements needed in a workout and to permit the nervous system to adapt accordingly. The process may be considered as an introductory period of sorts for helping a person to understand how movements work and how certain weights can be held.

2. Strength

This is to trigger the growth of new muscle mass. The person can start with smaller weights and eventually move on to larger ones depending on the progress of his or her efforts.

3. Power

Power focuses on how the body can manage more physical movements and actions in as short of a period of time as possible. Power makes it easier for a person to engage in certain functions and movements during a workout. The effort will help to maintain muscle mass and should not be utilized for trying to build further mass; the person may choose to build more muscle mass if desired, although that person may risk entering a plateau where no further results will come about.

The three stages require different types of exercises and certain standards for how long a set is to be and how much rest should be utilized between each set. Later on, this guide will discuss information regarding how well the body can handle certain exercises based on these stages.

Basic Considerations for Planning a Workout

Several factors have to be put into play during the training process:

Sets

A set is a series of repetitions of an exercise. A person has to complete enough of these repetitions to fill out a set. A set may use fewer repetitions during the stabilization process, although that number increases during the strength and power segments of a routine. For the best results, three sets of repetitions are needed. Fewer sets may be used in cases where the body is sensitive to certain actions; conversely, a person should avoid doing more than three sets at a time.

Repetitions (reps)

A repetition is a single movement that is produced within a certain workout routine. A person must complete a full range of motion in that movement. In some cases, the repetition will only entail one side of the body; the person must also repeat the same number of repetitions on the other side. The number of reps in a workout should be consistent with each set, although a person may remove or add one or two reps at a time. This may be based on a person's effort or ability to complete the task as required.

Exercise Selection

The selection of exercises in a routine can vary based on the ability of a person to complete them and how much that person is used to completing certain movements. A patient may be encouraged to work with the easiest exercises at the start and then progressively move on to more complicated ones. The SOAP method may be utilized for identifying a person's general ability to complete exercises, thus improving upon how well a workout routine may be planned. This is to ensure there are no concerns that may develop.

Tempo

The tempo involves the speed at which a person can complete repetitions. The tempo can be slow during the stabilization phase, as this is where the body is first becoming used to some of the movements. The tempo can be fastest in the power stage. At this point, it becomes easier for the body to manage large weights as quickly as possible.

Rest Period

A rest period is needed between each set to allow the body to recover. The body has to rest to prevent possible fatigue and also to allow the body to cool off. The rest period is generally listed at 60 seconds at the start, although that may be reduced down to 90 seconds as the participant moves forward in a program. The added timing is for the power stage, as this entails faster motions and sizeable weights. The timing should be brief, as too long of a rest period may result in the person failing to complete proper exercise movements later on.

Order of Exercises

The order of exercises should be planned with a participant's comfort in mind. The order of exercises may be planned out with the participant before the program begins. The best idea is to start with lighter exercises and eventually progress towards more complicated actions, including actions that need a greater range of motion or require extra weight for them to be completed accordingly. A person may be encouraged to focus on certain parts of the body at the start, depending on what he or she prefers to work with or a certain area of the body that a person wants to improve upon the most.

Volume

The volume of a workout refers mainly to the weight that would be lifted or the amount of resistance that the body can handle. The body must progress through the workout routine to handle more weight, and the total rate of progression should be planned so that a person doesn't struggle unduly.

Duration

The timing for a workout can vary, although it may be best to plan a workout at about 30 to 45 minutes on average. The total can expand to 60 minutes if needed. The duration may also be based on the frequency of the workout, such as every day or every other day, depending on what the participant needs. The training schedule must be planned cautiously. Excess effort may cause a higher risk of injury due to the added effort required.

Flexibility Training

Flexibility training focuses on how well a patient's range of motion may be supported. The practice entails helping the patient to manage his or her joint movements accordingly. There are three forms of flexibility training that may be covered in a program:

1. Corrective

Corrective practice consists of getting the range of motion in the joints to increase over time and correcting joint motions. This includes resolving possible muscle imbalances. A stretch in this practice is held for about 20 to 30 seconds at a time. The process helps the body become accustomed to the efforts required during a workout. Static stretching is strongly recommended, although self-myofascial release exercises may also work.

2. Active

The patient prepares the muscles for exercise routines. The muscles stretch while also being readied. The practice may also assist in releasing any excess amounts of stress within the body, thus allowing the participant to feel active and ready to workout. The patient moves a joint or muscle and stretches it through a full range of motion. The muscle is held in its final position for two seconds. The process can be repeated at least five times. Active-isolated and self-myofascial release exercises are recommended in this situation to increase a person's range of motion.

3. Functional

Functional flexibility refers to how soft tissues can be extended accordingly. This is a high-demand form of exercise. The joint moves through a full range of motion while a dynamic exercise is also completed. Dynamic stretching exercises are to be used in this situation. A self-myofascial release practice may also work for the patient's needs.

Autogenic vs. Reciprocal Inhibition

Inhibition occurs as muscles are inhibited from contracting during a stretching exercise. This comes as the Golgi tendon organ, or GTO, is activated. The GTO responds to tensions produced. The GTO is between the end of the muscle tissue and the tendon. It identifies tensions and inhibits motions. The spindle, in the end part of the muscle tissue, responds to the length of the muscle. The spindle produces a stretching sensation that the brain identifies. The process assists in managing proper coordination between the brain and the muscle.

Autogenic Inhibition: As a muscle contracts or stretches, the GTO starts working and inhibits a contraction while also contracting the antagonist or opposite muscle.

Reciprocal inhibition: The muscle spindle produces a reflexive contraction within the agonist muscle or stretch reflex. The antagonist muscle is relaxed at this point.

The agonist muscle relaxes during an autogenic process and contracts in a reciprocal action. The opposite can be said in a reciprocal process.

Self-Myofascial Release

The self-myofascial release process entails using slight amounts of pressure to break up knots and bends within the muscle tissue. The practice releases tension in the body and improves upon blood and lymphatic circulation. The effort helps improve upon the patient's range of motion and may increase that person's ability to move without inhibition. Foam rolling is utilized as a part of the self-myofascial release process. This helps with massaging the muscle tissue, allowing the muscles to feel sensations, thus improving upon how the body can stay active. This is an autogenic inhibition process.

Static Stretching

Static stretching is a practice where the patient takes a muscle to the point of tension. The stretch is held for about 30 seconds. The stretch causes the GTO and other mechanoreceptors to relax. This allows for an improved range of motion, helping to lengthen tighter muscles. The goal is to keep posture-related issues from developing. Static stretching focuses on autogenic inhibition.

Active-Isolated Stretching

Active-isolated stretches are held for up to two seconds. This is done at least five times. The process helps to lengthen muscles for short-term activities. This can work for tight muscles and works throughout the entire body. The exercise is a form of reciprocal inhibition.

Dynamic Stretching

Dynamic stretching works to increase the possible range of motion within a joint. Force is produced in the body to help improve upon the functionality of the tissue, thus improving upon how well the tissue is supported. This practice entails reciprocal inhibition.

Resistance Training

Resistance training is a practice that consists of the use of resistance or weights to train muscles. The practice helps with improving upon muscular contractions to build upon the patient's strength and endurance. This may also improve upon the size of the skeletal muscles when used accordingly. The specific plans that may be utilized in the resistance training process will entail the proper number of repetitions and a series of sets. Plans for working out in this situation should be planned accordingly.

Types of Sets

Multiple types of sets may be utilized in the workout process. These may be planned based on a person's fitness needs and how used to certain movements and actions he or she is.

Single Set

A single set involves one set of an exercise. This may entail a person using one set where a certain series of repetitions are used at a time. This is appropriate for beginners or for cases where a person has many types of exercises that he or she wishes to work on.

Multiple Set

A multiple-set routine involves using many sets of each exercise. For this, a patient will require a cool-off time between each set so the body can handle the movements involved.

Super Set

A super set involves two exercises performed quickly. There is very little rest involved in between each of these exercises.

Pyramid Set

The pyramid layout involves the amount of weight being used increasing or decreasing within each set. A patient who lifts weights may engage in a set with 120 pounds of resistance at the start, followed by a set with 140 pounds and then a third set with 160 pounds. The patient may go the other way around if desired.

Circuit Training

Circuit training is a practice where many exercises are performed together. This includes various types of exercises that focus on a very specific goal. The patient engages in at least one set for each exercise and does these all in a row, with very little rest between each exercise.

Circuit-training activities involve the following:

1. Strength

The practice focuses on weight-based activities that can involve free weights, body-weight actions and machine-based exercises.

2. Cardio

Cardiovascular circuit training concentrates on jumping jacks, jump squats and other quick exercises that may work with little to no equipment involved.

3. Combination

In this instance, a strength-based exercise is followed up by a cardio-based activity. Circuit training requires the participant to engage in activities without much rest. The person participating in this may use added flexibility exercises if desired, but the key is to help tone the muscles and to keep the body stable and strong.

Vertical Loading

Vertical loading involves varying one set to the next. The upper body is worked on first, followed by the lower body. After a set of exercises in the circuit is finished, the participant moves back to a new set where the upper body is worked on, followed by the lower. The person may work on the lower body first, although working on the upper body first is recommended.

Horizontal Loading

Horizontal loading entails all sets for a certain area of the body being worked upon before moving to the next area. For instance, a person might handle three sets of exercises on the upper body before going to three sets on the lower body.

Split Routine

A person may use a split routine where certain parts of the body are worked upon during certain days. The upper body may be worked upon on Mondays, Wednesdays and Fridays. Meanwhile, the lower body could be exercised on Tuesdays, Thursdays and

Saturdays. This is an example, although the participant can plan any schedule provided the workout is as evenly planned as possible.

Peripheral Heart Action

The peripheral heart action routine (PHA) involves upper and lower body workouts, alternating between one another, focusing upon improving circulation throughout the body.

Resistance Training Methods

The resistance training methods a person can participate in may be divided up between three phases. The phases listed here are included in order.

Stabilization

The first phase is the stabilization phase. This requires a 4/2/1 tempo that consists of four seconds for an eccentric contraction, two seconds for an isometric hold and one second for a concentric contraction. The slower motions allow for the body to become stable as connective tissue is formed. The practice prepares the muscles and the nervous system for added functions that may require more weight or an added amount of effort. More reps are used in a well-controlled environment. Some of the exercises that may be used in this period include:

- Push-ups
- Standing cable row
- Ball dumbbell chest press
- Ball squat with a curl to press emphasis
- Multiplanar step-up balance curl that moves to an overhead press
- Multiplanar step-up to balance
- Single-leg curls; this may work with dumbbells and barbells
- Seated military press; this should be ball-oriented

Strength

The second, third and fourth phases are strength training. As the body becomes stabilized, a 2/0/2 tempo can be used with a bit of extra weight. The reps are a little easier for the body to manage. The patient will use a full range of motion. The exercises to be used in this situation include:

- Lunge to two-arm dumbbell press
- Two-arm push press
- Barbell lifts; this includes a jerk and clean process
- Flat dumbbell chest press
- Seated cable row
- Barbell bench press
- Cable pushdowns
- Leg press
- Barbell squats
- Bicep curls; this may work with free weights or a machine
- Shoulder-press machine; this may work in a seated or standing form

Power

The fifth phase of the workout process involves power exercises. This works with a stronger tempo that is faster than the other phases and uses lighter weights. The practice works after the strength phases have helped to improve upon the body's muscles and strength. The moderate reps are used with lighter weights to tone the muscles and maintain them. A complete range of motion is required. The exercises that may be completed in this process include:

- Rotation chest pass
- Medicine ball chest pass
- Wood-chop throw
- Squat and tuck jumps
- Medicine ball side-throw
- Lightweight forms of the other exercises listed earlier may also be utilized

This process is to be handled last, after a person has worked on improving upon the body's structure, although this can work at any moment after certain goals for developing added bulk have been met.

Modalities for Resistance Training

Different devices may work for resistance training needs. Such devices are powered by different functions within the body.

Machines

A machine entails a weight that is placed on a fixed track. The design focuses on a layout where the user can adjust the weight to be lifted with a pin or cable-based material, although some larger weights may be added evenly onto the sides of a machine in some instances. A machine works mainly for the stabilization process to help a person understand how certain lifting motions work. The body gets used to the required motions in the process. However, synergist muscles that are needed for triggering larger amounts of weight may not be utilized as often when using such machines. A workout machine should only be used at the start of a lifting routine to help the patient get used to actions and to help prepare for strength-building routines.

Body Weight

Body-weight-oriented lifting processes often involve the use of resistance bands or cables. These are items that can be handled by a person with the intention of moving a band or cable out as far as possible. Part of this includes stretching items out to produce more tension, thus requiring more effort in the body to overcome any forces involved. The lifting process requires consistent tension on the body, thus allowing for muscles to be trained to handle intense amounts of pressure. Such items may be used in strength phases, although this may also work in the power phase as the patient is used to the heavy lifting processes that are required for overcoming certain weights.

Some body-weight exercises entail the use of medicine balls. These heavily-weighted balls may be lifted, tossed and handled in many positions to allow for the body's muscles to be trained. Other exercises can include push-ups, crunches and other actions that do not require any other outside materials. These exercises focus mainly on the efforts of the human body to handle natural weight. Some resistance bands or added weights may be included as needed.

Free Weights

Free weights are large weights that a person can lift in the strength phases, although they may also be used in smaller weight totals during the power phase. A free weight may include a barbell. This is used for managing both the left and right sides of the body, although this requires the weights on the two sides to be loaded up evenly. The added effort for balancing the weight and keeping it in place is vital for allowing the motor system in the body to function and develop.

When using a barbell, the patient must be trained well to handle the weight as evenly as possible. Failure to manage the weight evenly enough may cause the person to favor one side of the unit, thus putting the user at danger of further harm, depending on what one might do with the setup. Dumbbells are also used as popular weights for free weight needs. A dumbbell is a free weight that allows a person to lift weights with one side at a time. A dumbbell can include something that is held with one hand and will entail a certain amount of weight. Dumbbells are useful, provided that the user trains both sides of the body as evenly as possible.

Core-Training Exercises

The core muscles are the muscles that link to the LPHC. These muscles are required for the proper balancing and control of the patient's body. Among the muscles in the area include the gluteus medius, gluteus minimus, erector spinae and the internal and external obliques. Core-training exercises are needed for helping to keep the body stable and to allow for an appropriate muscle balance throughout the body. The stabilization must help to move forces within the body as evenly and carefully as possible.

The muscles that are to be trained are needed for safely producing concentric and eccentric functions. General stabilization is also supported by the core-training process to help with managing the body's regular actions. Muscles involved will link to the vertebrae for local stabilization. Muscles can also move from the pelvis to the spine to create a global stabilization setup. The appropriate exercises will ensure that the body stays active and healthy.

Stabilization

Stabilization exercises focus on how the spinal column and CNS may be stabilized during a workout.

Plank

The plank exercise involves the patient lying on the floor with his or her stomach to the ground. The steps are as follows:

1. Keep the weight on the elbows while putting them directly under the shoulders.
2. Move the legs outward and press into the heels.
3. Keep the core tight and pull the abs inward. The body should be kept in a straight line from top to bottom.
4. Hold the position for about 30 seconds. It can be held for up to 60 seconds as the person gets used to the exercise.

For cases where the routine is too difficult, the knees can be dropped down to the floor for extra support. However, the elbows should still support most of the patient's weight at this point.

Side Plank

The side plank concentrates on the same principle as the regular plank, but this is done on the person's side. The steps are as follows:

1. Lie on the side and keep the weight on the elbow directly over the shoulder.
2. Bend the knees by a small bit and move the hip off of the ground.
3. Hold for about 30 seconds. Make sure the hip stays off the ground.
4. Repeat for the other side.

Bird Dog

The leg is stretched back in the bird-dog routine, as follows:

1. Get on hands and knees and keep the spinal column in a straight line, from head to toe.
2. Lift the left arm and right leg up at the same time. Keep the right leg extended outward while the left arm is in front.
3. Hold for about five seconds.
4. Move back to the original position.
5. Repeat for about 10 to 15 reps.
6. Repeat for the other side.

Bridge

The bridge requires the participant to lie on his or her back while the knees are bent upward. The feet should be flat on the floor.

1. Lie down on the back and keep the knees bent upward. Feet must remain flat on the floor.
2. Lift the hips up toward the ceiling. This should produce a straight line from the knees to the shoulders.
3. Hold for about three to five seconds at the top part, eventually easing the body back down.

4. Repeat for about 10 to 15 reps.

Strength Training

The following exercises are designed to help people strengthen their core muscles. These may work with added weights, but in some cases the person's own body weight will be responsible for allowing the muscles to stay strong.

Reverse Crunches

A reverse crunch is an exercise that supports stability around the body.

1. Lie down on the back while keeping the knees together. Bend the legs back by about 90 degrees while the feet stay firm on the floor. Keep the palms facedown on the floor as well.
2. Tighten the abs and lift the hips off of the floor.
3. Crunch the knees inward towards the chest. Hold the position for a moment.
4. Lower the back down, but make sure the lower back does not arch or lose contact with the floor.

This practice can help with strengthening the core muscles quite well when 10 to 15 reps at a time are performed.

Ball Crunches

A ball crunch requires a person to lie down on a ball that is properly inflated. The inflation should help with keeping the body stable and steady so the person will not feel any discomfort.

1. Lie down with the lower back curvature on the inflatable ball. Keep the knees bent along the end part of the ball for the best results.
2. Lower the torso down while keeping the arms around the chest.
3. Raise the upper back and shoulders slightly. Keep the feet down and keep the ball stable and in the same position.
4. Lower the back and shoulders down.
5. Repeat for 10 to 15 reps.

Cable Rotations

A cable-core rotation exercise helps the body to handle a core motion with the use of a simple lever or other unit for quick lifting. This can work with added weights at the end of the cables to add extra resistance if desired.

1. Hold onto a cable with both hands on the right side. The left arm should be straight and stretched across the body.
2. Pull the cable towards the opposite side of the body. The right arm must be straight at the end.
3. Move the cable back to the starting position.
4. Repeat for about 10 reps.
5. Repeat the process with the hands on the left side and the right arm straight and stretched out.

Power Training

These next few exercises concentrate mainly on power-training functions. Many of these actions entail the use of a medicine ball. Medicine balls come in various weights and sizes. It's important to exercise caution and select a ball that is suitable for a person's needs and assessed range of motion.

Soccer Throw

A soccer throw works both abs and shoulders.

1. Hold a medicine ball in both hands.
2. Lift the ball up behind the head, holding it with both hands.
3. Take a step forward and then throw the ball towards a wall.
4. Pick the ball up and then repeat the same motion.
5. Alternate between each leg in terms of which one steps forward.
6. This practice may work for about 10 to 15 reps for each foot.

Rotation-Chest Pass

Another exercise with a medicine ball, the rotation-chest pass moves the body in a rotating manner while tossing the ball.

1. Stand with the body at a 90-degree angle towards a wall.
2. Keep the feet shoulder-width apart from each other.

3. Keep the medicine ball to the chest. The elbows should be flexed back.
4. Rotate the body while the glutes are contracted.
5. Keep the back leg pivoted while rotating.
6. Toss the ball towards the wall while rotating. The tossing motion should be completed after moving towards the wall in the workout.
7. Keep the shoulders straight and firm while holding and handling the ball.

This process can be used for a few reps, although this works best when alternating between the postures that are being practiced.

Medicine Ball Pullover Throw

This next option is used with a properly inflated stability ball.

1. Lie on a ball placed under the lower back. The knees must be bent at a right angle. The feet must also be flat on the floor and pointed forward.
2. Keep the medicine ball overhead.
3. Extend the arms all the way through.
4. Contract the glutes and keep the chin tucked in.
5. Crunch the body forward while throwing the medicine ball towards the wall.

This useful exercise can be handled with a few reps at a time, on each side. The patient should be used to the medicine ball before any of these exercises are to be used. A lightweight ball may also be used at the start; this may include a ball that is about five pounds in weight. Larger balls may also be used, although this might be risky depending on how used to the lifting process one is.

Additional Keys

Drawing-in maneuvers may be utilized in the core strengthening and training process. These exercises help get core stabilizers to move power towards the navel. The navel moves towards the spinal column in this process. The exercises listed above may help with allowing the navel to be drawn in towards the rest of the body for the best results. Bracing processes may also be utilized. This is where the abdominal muscles are contracted, and the lower back and glutes work together. This helps to stabilize the LPHC. About 60 to 90 seconds of rest should be planned in between each core set. The period can be around 45 to 60 seconds for strength or power exercises, although it is best to keep enough time in between sets so a person can safely recover and be prepared for the next set.

Balance Training

Balance training is a practice that focuses on helping to keep the body stable. This includes producing an added amount of awareness of one's balance and ability to stay stable. Balance training improves upon the body's ability to handle consistent muscle patterns where the joints are kept stable, and the muscles maintain a sense of control. The process entails a combination of eccentric and concentric motions. Eccentric motions involve a reduction in force while concentric actions involve the force being produced. These are designed to stabilize the core area and to support healthy neuromuscular systems.

Stabilization

The following exercises focus on basic stabilization efforts to keep the body active and ready to handle most basic balancing functions.

Single-Leg Balance

The single-leg balance helps improve upon how muscles can stay active while having a better reaction time.

1. Stand on one leg and lift the other leg toward a 12 o'clock position.
2. Swing the leg forward and back to the six o'clock position.
3. Repeat for 10 to 15 times on each leg.

Single-Leg Balance and Reach

The balance and reach exercise requires extra effort:

1. Keep the balancing leg bent by a slight bit. The hip should also be in line with the knee.
2. Draw the abs inward and tighten the glutes.
3. Keep the opposite leg straight and back at an angle. Keep the glute and calf muscles tightened.
4. Stabilize the area for about two seconds. Move the foot back toward the opposite part of the body.
5. About 10 to 15 reps of this exercise are needed on each leg for the best possible results.

Single-Leg Windmill

This action works well as a windmill activity that focuses on the person's weight to make it easier for the body to stay strong and active.

1. Stand on one leg to keep the body active.
2. Bend forward and push the legs back.
3. Lower the chest towards the floor. The positioning should be close to parallel to the surface.
4. Keep a mild bend around the knee.
5. Move the arms outward and keep them in line with the rest of the body.
6. Keep the position up and then rotate the torso. Move one hand down towards the toes and then twist to alternate the hands.
7. About 10 to 15 reps should be used at a time while working on each half.

Strength Training

Balance functions can be strengthened as well as possible. The muscles for balance, particularly along the legs, may be strengthened to help improve upon general balance efforts. The strength-training routines for balance will target the quads, glutes and hips.

Single-Leg Squat

This next exercise requires an extra bit of effort for moving the body up and down.

1. Place a box next to the body. The box should be up to the knee.
2. Stand on the right leg and hold a three- to five-pound-weight in each hand; the plates should be identical in design and weight.
3. Keep the hips back and bend the knee down to squat while raising the arms up. The key is to keep the weight balanced accordingly.
4. Lower down until the rear touches the box or the thigh is parallel with the floor. The arms need to be parallel to the floor as well while in front of the shoulders. The patient should not add lots of weight on the box or rest.
5. Move the foot forward and then straighten the knee. This will help with moving the body back up to the original starting position.
6. Repeat for eight to 15 reps on each side. This includes working evenly between the two legs, with the same number of reps favoring each leg.

The back should be kept as straight as possible.

Single-Leg Deadlift

The single-leg deadlift exercise requires added weights in one hand. A kettlebell is strongly recommended here.

1. Hold a kettlebell in one hand, to the side.
2. Stand on the leg next to the hand that the kettlebell is being held on.
3. Bend the knee slightly. Perform a deadlift by bending on the hip and extending the leg behind, for balance.
4. Lower the kettlebell down until the body is parallel on the ground.
5. Move the bell back to the upright position.

This can be used for as many repetitions as one wishes, although a routine from 10 to 15 reps may be good enough.

Lunge to Balance

The lunge-to-balance routine is very easy to follow:

1. Stand with the feet wide to the hips.
2. Step forward with a basic lunge.
3. Keep the core muscles tight while the hands are on the hips.
4. Lower the body down to where the back knee is an inch above the ground. The front knee should be at a near-right angle.
5. Push upward to a standing position while the front leg moves up in the air with the same right-angle position. The back leg should be used for balance.
6. Hold the position for a few seconds.
7. Move the front leg back for a lunge.

This can be used with multiple repetitions on one side before moving on to the next leg and completing the same number of repetitions at that point.

Power Training

Power-training activities may also be utilized for keeping the body healthy and active. The process for moving forward should be handled carefully.

Single-Leg Box Hop-Up

This first exercise for power training requires the use of a small box to help with improving upon how the leg muscles for balance are triggered and stabilized.

1. While facing the box, stand with the feet straight ahead.
2. Bend the knees down and then move one leg off of the ground next to the other leg.
3. Squat downward and move up with the body propelling its weight to land on the box.
4. Bend the knees while on the box. This helps to contract the glutes to stabilize the body at this point.
5. Hold for about three to five seconds. The body needs to ensure it is fully stable at this point.
6. Step down to the original position and repeat the motion.

This can be done with the same number of reps with each leg being favored in the process.

Single-Leg Box Hop-Down

This process may be seen as a reverse of the hop-up.

1. Keep one leg off of the box while standing on it. The leg should be bent slightly up.
2. Jump down off of the box while moving at a 90-degree angle.
3. Keep the leg bent at the same angle. The other leg should land gently on the floor.
4. The arms can be stretched out from the rest of the body during the entire exercise process. The arms should be parallel to the floor in this case.
5. Repeat for the same number of reps on each side.

This works best when the box is at a small height. About six inches is enough for adding a challenge and still keeping the process safe. The box in question should be solid and not cushioned so the surface will not be a slipping hazard.

Multiplanar Single-Leg Hop

This strength exercise does not require a box for use, although that can be added into the exercise if desired.

1. Move a leg up, with the knee bent upward. Try to keep the knee bent at a right angle if possible.
2. Keep the hands at the waist and hips.
3. Move the leg that was up back and into a straight position.
4. While the original leg is moved to be straight, the other leg should be bent with a right angle.
5. Repeat the motion again with the other leg being bent up properly.
6. Repeat for as many reps as desired, but be sure the number of reps is consistent among both legs.

Reactive (Plyometric) Training

Reactive or plyometric training is a process where the body engages in a series of quick movements with eccentric contraction in mind. The contractions are quickly followed up by concentric contractions. The process focuses on increasing the power or strength of a person and the speed at which that strength is conveyed. The main goal of plyometric training is to help strengthen the body and make it move faster. This works well for managing the body and keeping it functional in most situations. The stabilization is also needed for ensuring the body can stay active. The amortization, or transition phase of the process, must be managed. This is a transition between the eccentric and concentric actions. The transition has to be as fast as possible. A faster movement results in a more powerful concentric action.

Three Vital Stages

Three stages are evident in plyometric training:

1. Eccentric

Energy is stored within the muscle to prepare the body.

2. Amortization

Muscles are stabilized as they take in the energy needed to complete a movement.

3. Concentric

The energy within the muscle can now be relieved.

Stabilization

Many plyometric actions focus on triggering the stabilizing muscles around the body.

Box Jumps

The box jump is a common exercise in plyometrics.

1. Set up a box that is about six inches high.
2. Lower into a squatting position; keep the feet shoulder-width apart from one another.
3. Squat down and move up with the entire body.
4. Land on the box with the balls of the feet.
5. Step back down and reset the body position back to the beginning.
6. Complete for ten reps. Try to do three sets if possible.

This exercise can also be completed with added weights to increase the challenge involved or to try and make the exercise more interesting.

Skater Jump

The skater jump places an emphasis on the glutes and quads. The full load is placed on one leg.

1. Bend down into a squat position. Keep the feet close to one another while also favoring the weight on the right leg.
2. Push off the right leg. Push on the opposite side.
3. Land on the left leg; do not be too rough.
4. Move the right leg behind the left leg.
5. Repeat the exercise with the left leg.
6. Continue the process with ten reps. One rep will start with the right leg and then go on to the left leg.

This should be done with three sets if possible. The exercise can also be handled with the arms moving to the sides while the exercise takes place. The movement involved can be handled accordingly.

Multiplanar Jumps with Stabilization

This is more of a hopping exercise, but it is vital for helping the body to stay active and to allow for a better sense of movement.

1. Stand straight with feet hip-width apart.
2. Suck the midsection towards the spine.
3. Start balancing on the left leg.
4. Hop forward with the left leg while landing on the right foot.
5. Balance for about three to four seconds.
6. Jump back to land on the left foot.
7. Keep the balance for a few more seconds.
8. Start the process but with the right leg being used at the start.

The process can work for three sets of 10 reps, provided the left and right legs are both worked.

Strength

These strength-based exercises may be utilized with optional added weights on the legs.

Butt Kicks

The butt kick is a practice that focuses on the glutes.

1. Stand with the shoulders wide apart, face forward.
2. Kick the feet up with the heels touching the glutes. Kick them up one at a time.
3. Pump the arms as the feet are kicked up.
4. Keep repeating for ten times in a set. This works best when handled with three sets.

Tuck Jumps

The tuck jump requires the person to bend down to complete the process.

1. Stand with the feet shoulder-width apart. Keep the hands on the side.
2. Keep the spine up while the abs are tight.

3. Move the shoulders back while the belly is pushed in.
4. Squat down with the knees at a right angle.
5. Move the hips back and move forward. Make sure the back is flat and straight.
6. Push down while making a jumping motion.
7. Keep the knees around the chest and grab the knees with the hands.
8. Be sure to land gently and avoid excess stress on knee joints.
9. When landing, stay on the middle part of the feet.
10. Use ten reps with three sets.

Squat Jumps

The squat jump is another move that can be easy to complete if planned out right.

1. Stand with the feet shoulder-width apart.
2. Start with a regular squat movement.
3. Jump up with the core muscles tightened.
4. Go back to the squat position after landing.
5. Complete for ten reps with three sets.

The entire foot needs to be utilized. The shoulders must not lean beyond the knees as that might cause excess straining along the back.

Power

Power-based exercises are needed for helping to use all of a person's strength in as little time as possible. These exercises are recommended for those who have experience with such exercises and are ready to progress in their workouts.

Box-Run Steps

Box-run steps are utilized to help move the muscles quickly while triggering more muscle groups.

1. Face a six-inch box.
2. Keep one foot on top of the box.
3. Start by quickly alternating your feet on the box (in a sort of prancing motion).

4. The arms are to move back and forth while the motion is made.

Ice Skaters

Another fast-motion move, this one works on the quads. The motions are similar to what one might notice when ice skating.

1. Keep the feet shoulder-width apart.
2. Look forward with the chest up, and the back straight.
3. Jump towards the right and bend the knees slightly.
4. Reach down and move toward the outside part of the right foot with the left hand moving forward.
5. Complete the same movement but on the other side.
6. Complete this motion quickly, but keep a sense of balance.

This movement is just like speed skating.

Additional Points

The rest periods between sets will vary depending on the exercises. The resting period can be up to 60 seconds between sets for strength and power exercises. For stabilization efforts, the rest period can be up to 90 seconds in length. The stabilization exercises are to be completed at the start, thus making those exercises consistent with others that one might engage in. The basic workout routine to use in this case is as follows:

1. **Stabilization.** The key part entails control and ensuring the small sets of five to eight reps are completed properly. This includes 90-second resting periods.
2. **Strength.** The repeating motions can work with up to ten reps, with a 60-second resting period in between each set.
3. **Power.** Move as fast as possible. This includes working with twelve reps at a time, in a set with 60 seconds in between each set.

Proprioceptive Plyometrics

Proprioceptive plyometrics should be planned based on a patient's general sense of balance and stability.

Manipulation

Manipulation requires a person to use different positions and situations for completing workouts. Manipulation helps to improve upon how well a patient can handle certain exercises while triggering the body into handling certain connections based on a person's actions.

Proprioceptive plyometrics can entail many types of manipulation efforts. Each uses different principles based on maintaining how well the nervous system can recall the movements that have to take place in the workout:

1. **Balancing**

Balancing exercises are recommended for helping the patient to maintain a healthy sense of equilibrium. The balance efforts can be handled on various slopes, although sometimes it is best to challenge the body into maintaining the same position on a certain surface for as long as possible.

2. **Exercises with the Eyes Closed**

Many of the plyometric exercises listed here can be completed while the patient's eyes are closed. This helps with allowing the brain to create appropriate links for how certain physical activities are to be handled. The goal is to allow the brain and muscles to be connected properly. The participant can start working out with the eyes open and then progress to having the eyes closed. The practice improves upon how well a person can handle the motions involved with a workout.

3. **Basic Strengthening Exercises**

Standard strengthening exercises can come in many forms. These include exercises for triggering muscle fibers to improve upon a person's overall strength levels.

4. **Nodding Head**

The nodding-head effort requires the patient to nod his or her head while engaging in certain workout routines. This creates a sense of slight disorientation that requires the person to maintain his or her balance while keeping control of the muscles responsible for that balance.

5. **Single-Leg Stand**

Standing on only one leg when exercising teaches the brain to create new connections that focus on how well a person can stay stable and active.

Standing Progression

There are four standing positions that can train the muscles:

1. Two legs on a stable surface
2. One leg on a stable surface

3. Two legs on an unstable surface

4. One leg on an unstable surface

The participant can move from the first point to the next and so forth, as he or she becomes comfortable.

Additional Materials for Proprioceptive Manipulation

Various added materials may be added to the proprioceptive process. These are to be organized from the most stable to the least stable:

1. Floor

2. Balance beam

3. Foam roll

4. Foam pad

5. Balancing disk

6. Wobble board

7. Stability ball

A person should start working on exercises on the floor and then move on down the list towards the most unstable materials. The key is to keep the workout movements more challenging without forcing the participant into the most complicated process too soon.

Speed, Agility and Quickness Training

Speed, agility and quickness training (SAQ) training focuses on the body's ability to react to certain forces. This includes being able to accelerate and stop on a dime. The overall goal is to keep the body stable. These are three elements of SAQ routines:

1. **Speed**

Speed is vital. It's the measure between the length of a stride and how long it takes for that stride to be completed.

2. **Agility**

The agility measurement is a review of the effort a person puts in toward starting, stopping and changing direction. The key is to maintain posture while working out.

3. Quickness

Quickness refers to how well a person can change position while maintaining the highest force or power output possible.

SAQ Tests

Resisted Sprints

Resisted sprints consist of a person running while carrying extra weight. The material will add resistance that requires a person to put extra effort into the sprinting process. Some items that may be carried for additional weight include resistance bands, a parachute, a sled or a resistance belt. The practice assists in triggering more muscle fibers and can improve upon the hip extensor muscles. The added neural functionality also triggers the body into putting in an extra bit of effort for running. Any resistance that is added should also only be planned after the surface is reviewed for stability.

Cone Drills

Cone drills require the participant to run through a short track and to move across a series of cones. A person might have to move around one cone after a brief sprint, pull off another sprint and then move around yet another cone. The track for a cone drill can be laid out as one sees fit, but enough room must be added to allow the participant to move through the cones well while providing a better range of motion. This practice may also help with improving upon one's general functionality.

Agility Ladder Drills

Agility or speed-ladder drills are often encouraged to help people train their reflexes and ability to respond to quick stimuli. In this, a rope ladder is placed on the ground. A runner uses a quick series of motions to keep his or her feet within the ladder or around in. Some ladder drills require a person to alternate his or her feet inside each ladder rung. The process can include resistance bands or can even incorporate a jump rope or other items to add to the challenge. Either way, the practice helps to train the patient's agility and to improve acceleration and deceleration while also shifting directions.

Cardiorespiratory Training

Proper cardiorespiratory training is needed for improving upon both how well the body responds to a workout and how much effort a person can put into the workout routine in general.

Stages and Heart-Rate Zones

Multiple stages may be used in the cardiorespiratory process to help improve upon how well the body can handle various actions. Cardio activities will help the body to adapt to many motions and functions.

There are three stages:

Stage I

The first stage entails the body building upon cardio efforts. This is useful for basic individual efforts and can work to start an initial workout routine. The first stage is for helping a person to engage in lighter activities that are not too hard to manage. The efforts should start slowly and carefully. About 30 to 60 minutes of exercise should be used here. The first heart-rate zone should be used in this case. This entails getting the heart rate to 65 to 75 percent of a person's maximum. Stage I activities include walking, jogging and yoga practice.

Stage II

The second stage focuses on people who have engaged in low-impact cardio activities. The goal is for a person to get ready to work at a higher intensity level. The second heart-rate zone, of 76 to 85 percent of a person's maximum rate, is to be attained here. The first zone will be incorporated during the recovery process. A work/rest ratio of 1:3 is needed. One minute of work in the second heart-rate zone will be followed by three minutes in the first zone. Over time, the person can work hard enough to attain a 1:1 ratio. That is, the patient will feel more comfortable and confident with his or her workout routine. At this juncture, the person is ready for the third stage. Group classes are commonplace among Stage II practices. These include step and spinning classes. Kickboxing and other aerobic actions may also be incorporated.

Stage III

The cardio training involved in Stage III is more intense and focuses mainly on proper athletic performance. The third heart-rate zone, which entails 86 percent or more of a person's MHR, is to be attained in this case. The second zone is for recovery, while the first zone is for cooling down. Stage III practices include sprinting and other cardio actions that require a larger amount of effort.

Timing for Stages

For the best results, a participant must time the stages being utilized accordingly. Stage III may be attained once a week, but it should not be used more than that or else it may be difficult for the patient to recover from the workout. During the rest of the week, a person may alternate between Stages I and II. The layout of these stages can be planned to one's liking, provided enough effort is put into play.

Interval

Interval training is a common part of cardio training that entails a person working with a certain amount of effort within a brief moment of time. Interval training may entail the following activities:

- Cycling
- Rowing
- Running
- Climbing stairs
- Rope jumping
- Calisthenics

Any action that requires regular motion can be used in interval training. The key is to produce a series of rest periods in between sessions, based on the participant's ability to handle the exercises being recommended. The process can also substitute high- and low-intensity training positions as desired. Patients are encouraged to be cautious and to incorporate proper resting periods. Excess activity during interval training routines can cause mechanical damage around the muscles and may cause intense fatigue.

Steady State

Steady-state training focuses on producing a consistent amount of effort when working out. The speed is static during the entire session, although this can work in a low or moderate pace rather than something faster, such as what may be noticed in interval training. Many of the same activities used in interval training can be utilized, but they should be slower or less intense in. The process may produce consistent results while also staying under a person's respiratory threshold. The participant should feel more comfortable during the workout process thanks to the body not being forced into more stress or undue effort than necessary. This practice may not be appropriate for those aiming to build upon their aerobic capacities or those who are aiming to lose weight. While steady-state training can help with these goals, it will take a significant amount of time for a person to reach a goal in any situation.

Warming Up

The warm-up process is designed to support the body and to help prepare the tissues. Many stretching exercises are designed as warm-up processes for more intensive procedures, although some lighter exercises may also count as warm-up routines. A general warm-up process that focuses on getting the entire body ready may be utilized. A specific process that targets a very specific part of the body may also be used if needed. The plan for warming up should be organized based on the area that will be worked upon and how much effort will go into a workout.

Cool-Down Processes

The cool-down process entails resting the body after an exercise period is fully complete. This is to reduce the patient's heart rate to a nominal total and to also prevent blood from adding up in the extremities. The body's temperature will return to a normal level. The muscle length will also go back to a normal rate, thus ensuring the body can recover properly and effectively.

Progression and Regression in Exercises

Progressions in exercises refer to times when additional movements or actions may be incorporated into a routine. Progressions may be added into a workout based on how well a person is completing that routine and whether that someone can physically handle the new movements being added. The efforts may also work in cases where the patient understands how well the body is to move. However, a person must avoid anything overly complicated.

Regressions entail cases where part of an exercise is dropped. This may include a reduction in the number of reps involved or a person dropping a specific motion or amount of weight used in the workout routine. Such a move can be used in cases where a person is engaging in certain actions and might not be capable of handling them as well as he or she has previously done. Progressions and regressions will vary by each exercise. The patient should be consulted to see how well he or she can handle the exercises or whether there is a risk of possible injury later on.

General Adaptation Syndrome

General adaptation syndrome develops when a person responds to certain stressors and actions within a workout. The syndrome can be measured with one of three stages in mind.

Alarm Reaction

The first reaction to a stressor is the alarm reaction. This alarm will cause protective functions to develop within the body.

At this point:

- The adrenal gland releases cortisol.
- The heart rate starts to increase.
- The cortisol eventually causes adrenaline to rise, thus increasing the body's energy.

The alarm reaction can start within a few moments following a sudden event or incident.

Resistance Development

As the body recognizes the stressor, it begins to adapt. The resistance development process keeps the stressor from being too significant or harmful. The following things may occur during the resistance stage:

- The body's heart rate starts returning to its normal state.
- Cortisol continues to be released, although it takes a bit for this to be controlled.
- A person may become irritable due to the new stimulus.
- It may be difficult for a person to concentrate or be aware of what is in an area.

Exhaustion

The stressor will usually disappear after a while. Any stressor that persists will cause exhaustion to settle in. In this case, the stressor will become too intense for a person to handle, increasingly the risk of injury or excess fatigue. A patient may develop the following symptoms:

- Depression may start to settle in due to the ongoing physical and emotional pressure.
- Anxiety may develop
- The patient's stress-tolerance levels may start to decline.
- Burnout will settle in after a while. At this point, the person will become too tired to continue working on a certain type of action.

When Can General Adaptation Syndrome (GAS) Occur?

General Adaptation Syndrome (GAS) can develop at any point in one's life. This may come about due to physical problems or medical issues. But in some cases, GAS can develop due to family-related issues or other personal matters.

The key part of GAS is to quickly find ways to measure stress. Failing to get beyond the stress may result in the body experiencing added fatigue or a lack of a desire to keep on working out. A patient may also develop a weaker immune system as a result, thus causing the person to become more susceptible to infections and other significant diseases.

Vital Principles of Working Out

Specificity

The principle of specificity refers to how well a patient can adapt to certain demands on the body. The body must know how to adapt to changes if the person is to be safe and protected. The concept may also be referred to as the SAID or Specific Adaptation to Imposed Demands principle. These aspects of specificity may be noticed:

1. **Mechanical**

The weight and movements that are added to the patient's body must be identified and recognized. The patient has to know what can be done to manage those new movements and must be taught to adapt to how they work.

2. **Neuromuscular**

The speed of the contractions that are produced must be explored alongside the exercises that are to be utilized.

3. **Metabolic**

The energy that is added to the body must also be reviewed. Metabolic specificity refers to how well the body can handle the newfound energy demand that has been added to it, thus allowing the body to stay functional and capable of handling more motions.

Overload

The principle of overload occurs as the stimulus that one works with can produce a better result if planned accordingly. Specifically, the stimulus must be greater than that of what a person can handle at the moment. For instance, the principle of overload would suggest that a person who wants to lift weights must lift weights that are a little greater than what he or she is used to handling in order to gain muscle mass. Through regular training and functionality, it becomes easier for the muscles to grow and for the nervous system to recognize those weights. By using these weights consistently, it becomes easier for the body to respond well and stay active while becoming stronger.

Variation

Another principle that may be utilized involves variation. The process helps to improve upon overload while also keeping a person from being exhausted. In this case, a person will complete an extended variety of exercises. These include multiple exercises that target different parts of the body. Some of these may also require multiple types of movements; this can include a mix of both weight-training exercises for the legs and treadmill running.

The practice improves upon how well the body can workout while allowing the body to adapt to more movements and exercises. The practice may also reduce stress and eliminate the risk of burnout. The effort involved should be planned ahead of time for the best results. This includes reviewing what can be done to see how the body can respond and feel comfortable with the movements. The participant may also become mentally prepared for more activities while feeling comfortable with the actions being planned out.

Periodization

Periodization is a process for planning a workout routine that focuses on a series of specific periods. Many training adaptations may be planned out during the routine to improve upon the participant's ability to workout accordingly. The periods that are used should entail the same forms of stabilization, strength and power exercises. These are to be planned to allow for a more comprehensive approach to working out, keeping the body active and ready.

Linear and Undulating Periods

The periodization process can entail a linear or undulating period. The process works with different practices based on what a person can handle. In a linear period, a person will engage in activities in this manner:

1. A single phase, where a person engages in stabilization exercises, may be planned.
2. After a few weeks, that person will begin a strength-training program.
3. In another couple of weeks, that person moves into the power stage of the program.

The linear nature of this shows that a person will move from the basic lifting processes involved to something that focuses more on strength.

An undulating period focuses on the intensity of workouts, changing by the day. For instance:

1. On Monday, a person will participate in stabilization exercises.
2. A few days later, on Wednesday, the person will do the strength segment of the workout.
3. On Friday, that person will focus on power exercises.
4. The routine can be repeated next week.

The undulating process allows for an extended approach to working out while still offering a consistent amount of rest and recovery time.

How Long Does the Plan Last For?

The period can vary based on the needs that a participant has. A phase may last for four to six weeks at a time. Meanwhile, an undulating practice can work for eight to twelve weeks. Cycles may be planned on a weekly, monthly or annual basis. These cycles are respectively known as microcycles, mesocycles and macrocycles. The cycle may be planned with a trainer as needed based on a person's workout goals and any short or long-term desires one has for a healthier body.

FITTE Principle

The FITTE Principle focuses on five specific points for the effectiveness of a workout:

1. Frequency

The frequency refers to the number of training activities that a person enters into during a given time period. This may include a person looking for a certain number of workouts in a week or month. A person might be encouraged to workout once a day or every other day. A plan may be used to figure out what one can do when working out.

2. Intensity

The intensity entails the general effort that a person puts into the body. This includes a review of how well the body can handle its efforts. The intensity can be measured based on the patient's heart rate. A patient that puts in a workout that goes from 65 to 95 percent of one's MHR will enter into an appropriate routine that puts in enough pressure and effort on the body while still allowing the patient to recover after a period of time. The key is to keep the patient from experiencing feelings of breathlessness or extreme exhaustion.

3. Time

The time involves how long a person will be engaged in a certain activity within a particular period. In most cases, a patient will need about 30 minutes of working out at a time, five days a week.

4. Type

The type is the kind of activity that one engages in during a workout. It may involve various basic health actions like climbing up the stairs, mowing one's lawn or other forms of yardwork.

People looking to increase their fitness levels may engage in more intensive types of activities. Such actions may involve treadmill use, sporting activities and weight training, among other actions that are more strenuous and require an extra bit of physical effort.

5. Enjoyment

The patient's enjoyment is critical to the success of a workout program. A patient must experience a positive feeling during the workout and have a desire to continue. The actions used in the four other points in the FITTE Principle should match up with the desires or interests that the participant has so it becomes easier for the patient to get in a good workout while remaining positive.

Risk vs. Reward

The risks and rewards of an activity should be analyzed to identify whether a certain routine should be planned.

Risks

The risks that come with certain routines involve:

- The risk of an acute injury
- The potential for injuries caused by excessive use
- The amount of stress involved being too high
- The possible tension that may be triggered during the workout routine

Rewards

Various added rewards may come about during certain workout functions:

- The body's strength or flexibility may improve
- A person can be motivated to continue to work toward improving his or her body

- A person may also become more confident while performing certain actions

The patient should be consulted regarding how a routine is to be planned. The patient's plans should be laid out based on the risks and the possible rewards. The person may be given the final say about a certain routine, although this point may be countered based on any possible observations by the CPT.

Overtraining

Overtraining is a dangerous activity where the body tries to workout beyond one's natural ability to recover. A person who engages in overtraining may experience the following concerns:

- A reduction in the quality of one's performance
- Fatigue
- Changes in hormones
- A loss of appetite
- A reduction in one's immune system, thus resulting in an increased risk of infections or illnesses
- Changes in one's sleeping habits; this includes possibly not getting enough sleep

Proper rest and recovery parameters must be planned to avoid overtraining. Time limits may also be established to reduce the risk of overtraining.

Joint Dysfunction

Joint dysfunction is a threat that may develop due to overtraining or from a lack of rest. The concern occurs as the sensory input produced is not consistent with what the body is trying to attain. In this case, the wrong motor response is produced. The muscle will become inhibited as a result. The joint dysfunction issue will cause incorrect movement patterns due to muscle inhibition, thus causing possible injuries. The added swelling and inflammation that develops may result in changes to one's proprioception.

Rest and Recovery

The body must rest and recover following a workout to allow the body to heal and to prevent the risk of any added fatigue caused by the effort involved.

A person may spend a day in between workouts to allow the body to recover.

Several points may also be added to the rest and recovery process:

1. Allow for a proper amount of sleep in between workout sessions.

This includes enough sleep in the evening to allow the body to naturally heal itself. The sleep must take place at night, in a natural setting. A person in a cooler environment may have an easier time with restoring his or her body while sleeping.

2. Hydration is vital during the recovery process.

Hydration helps to restore the fluids that are lost in the workout process. Water is the best option, although sports drinks with electrolytes may be utilized immediately after working out to restore fluids.

3. A healthy diet is required for recovery.

A dietician may be consulted for additional help.

4. The patient's posture must be supported well.

The posture can work with support for standing and sitting with one's back straight while also avoiding leaning to the side.

5. Regular stretching is also encouraged throughout the day.

Stretching helps to keep the body from feeling stiff or worn out. This is particularly vital for those whose joints might have become worn out from all the movements made during a workout routine.

Trends in Training Programs

Various trends have developed in training programs to make them more unique and potentially useful for many people. A CPT can consider using these in a program to make it easier for people to want to continue working out while making the most of their routines.

Fitness Trackers

People these days frequently using fitness trackers to make it easier for them to stay active and healthy. Part of this includes reviewing how often one engages in certain physical actions and what can be done to stay active. A fitness tracker may be incorporated into one's workout to review how well that person is improving upon a routine. In some cases, the tracker may work with certain goals that are to be attained over time.

Social Media

Social media avenues are growing in prominence. These include places where people can talk with one another online, discussing all the various aspects of daily life, including fitness. A CPT can link up to a fitness patient through social media. Patients may also talk with each other to share ideas and plans and to work together towards attaining certain goals for fitness, strength training and weight loss. The CPT should also share information with those people about what they can do when working out. This can include adding regular tips or reminders to participants. Encouragement can also be provided to people on social media to help them stay motivated and interested in the workout routines that they are entering into.

Mobile Apps

Mobile applications on tablets and smartphones may be utilized to help people participate in various fitness routines. A mobile app can provide information on one's workout and offer guidance for a person to follow while on the go. These can be especially good for people in between training or workout sessions. People can also use these mobile apps to record information on what they are doing in their workouts and lifestyle routines.

Technology For Use

Some of the items that may be used in the workout process include the following:

Heart-Rate Monitor

A heart-rate monitor may be used to help a patient identify how well his or her heart is working during a routine. This entails the use of a vest that links up to a mobile device or wearable performance tracker. The monitor works better than a plain performance tracker as the larger tracker is in direct contact with the areas around the heart and may offer a larger range of coverage.

Performance Tracker

A performance tracker is a device that a person wears on his or her wrist or another part of the body. This tracks:

- The amount of steps a person takes in a day
- Average pulse throughout the day
- Speed at which a person is moving about throughout the day
- Any periods of sedentary activity

- How well a person sleeps; this includes an analysis of sleep cycles and when REM sleep is attained

The performance tracker may link to a smartphone or other device to review how well a person's physical activities are working. The data recorded can be compared with a person's established goals. The information on a performance tracker will guide a person towards attaining a healthier lifestyle, although this is in no way meant to replace a regular workout routine.

Calorie Counter

A calorie counter is a device that may be used to analyze how well a patient is maintaining a healthy diet. The counter is designed as a program that may work on a mobile device to figure out what one is eating. The program works in the following manner:

1. A person records information on the type of food he or she consumes. This includes when that person had the food, how large the portion was and how the food was prepared.
2. The program analyzes the input and figures out the number of calories.
3. The program then tallies the total number of calories that were consumed in the day.

The key part of the program is to identify how well a person can handle a regular dietary routine. The person must show a general capability for handling diet the right way. Part of this includes being able to eat within a certain caloric limit. Failing to adhere to proper caloric standards may cause a person to struggle to lose weight or build muscle mass. The calorie counter may help encourage a person to make smarter decisions over what he or she is eating.

Considerations for Special Populations

Seniors

A senior's training program should work with controlled activities that entail a sense of basic support for the body to prevent possible falls. A stationary bicycle or a treadmill that uses secure handrails and stepping spaces may be utilized. Underwater activities may also be utilized to improve upon the body's range of motion, thus preventing possible issues relating to arthritic joints. Cardiorespiratory activities can be performed about three to five times a week. The routines should be gentle; about 85 percent of one's VO2MAX can be used at the most. The practice can also work for about 30 to 60 minutes, although this can work in eight- or 10-minute intervals if necessary.

Any progression that is to be made should be done slowly. All exercises should be gentle, comfortable and monitored appropriately. Regular breathing is also recommended so as to avoid any lightheadedness. Dynamic stretches may also be encouraged. Lightweight stabilization exercises can also be used for stability training if desired. This is only to be used in cases where the patient feels an ability to handle the weights involved. Further resistance training stages can be entered into only if the person has managed to handle the proper posture for such actions.

Youth

A younger person may engage in sports activities and various physical games. Running and jogging activities can also be encouraged. The activities should be handled for at least five days in the week. The exercises should last 60 minutes a day. The key part of a program for youths is to make it work based on how well the patient's posture can be controlled. Part of this includes ensuring the body feels energetic, and the participant remains interested in regular physical activity. The process of working out is intended to be fun and enjoyable for all people. Resistance training can work two or three days in a week, but this must only work for the stabilization period. Strength training is only for mature adolescents based on how well their postures are controlled and whether a physician recommends such physical actions.

Prenatal

Any motions that a pregnant woman enters into should be gentle and low impact. Underwater exercises may be encouraged. Stationary biking can also work, provided the body is placed in an appropriate position during the routine. Stage I cardiovascular activities can also be considered. A pregnant woman should not engage in anything more intense than this unless a physician agrees. The activity can work for 15 to 30 minutes at a time, three to five days a week. Resistance training can work with lighter loads and should focus on stabilization only. The training may work two or three times a week. The exercises that may be used will be reduced in intensity based on how far into the pregnancy the woman is.

Obese Patients

Obese patients are encouraged to engage in low-impact activities, including rowing and treadmill walking. Aquatic exercises may also work for those who have experienced a reduction in their rates of motion. The person should be active with consistent cardiovascular activities at least five days in a week. Workouts can go for about 40 to 60 minutes in a day. The program can be stretched out into two even sessions during the day. The result should entail the patient getting from 60 to 80 percent of one's VO2MAX. The first and second phases of strength or resistance-training routines can be encouraged at this point, two or three times in a week. A patient should complete activities while sitting or standing, to ensure his or her comfort. The general goal for obese patients is to gradually introduce them into the process for losing weight. This is to keep the body from experiencing more pressure and reduce the risk of any possible injuries.

Diabetics

Those with diabetes may require resistance training with one to three sets of 10 to 15 reps about two or three times in a week. A patient's glucose control must be monitored regularly. Exercise may improve upon insulin sensitivity, thus allowing a person to use his or her own insulin. The process may reduce the body's dependency on medications for controlling diabetes or at least make those medications more effective in how they are used.

A participant's feet must also be monitored regularly. Blisters and other forms of trauma may be dangerous for diabetics due to the risk of infection. The feet of diabetic patients are more sensitive to injuries and possible amputation due to the nerves in the area being affected. Flexibility exercises are strongly encouraged among diabetics. Any other exercises for diabetics may be consistent with what is recommended among obese patients.

Patients with Hypertension

About 10 to 20 reps of resistance training can work for one to three sets, two or three times a week. The weights used should not be overly heavy. The stabilization process of lifting is recommended with light strength routines involved, although the efforts should be gentle on the body. Excess weights may trigger significant medical issues relating to hypertension. A patient's body position must be observed cautiously, with an emphasis on confirming that a person's body is in the right angle and is not pronating or shifting. Changes in position might directly influence the patient's blood pressure response. Any progress that is to be made should be handled slowly, so the patient is not forced into more stress than necessary. A person should be allowed to get up gently. Any cases where someone rises too fast may cause significant health concerns.

Arthritis Patients

People with arthritis should use fewer reps in their workouts. About 10 to 12 reps can be utilized. Heavy weights must also be avoided. Such weights may trigger further harm around the patient's tissues. A person's range of motion should be examined carefully. A person should be allowed to only move at the right range of motion based on what someone can work with. About five to ten minutes of exercise can be used at the start. As the patient becomes used to the exercise routine, the amount of time spent working out can eventually increase.

Osteoporosis Patients

While resistance training may be utilized among osteoporosis patients, the weight that may be lifted should be less than 85 percent of one's maximum weight for realistic lifting, if possible. The effort is to tone muscles and to keep them stabilized while keeping the bones from being at risk of fractures. About 10 to 12 reps may be used in lifting, with one to three sets, two to three times a week.

All exercises are based on how well a patient may manage his or her posture. The patient should be progressed towards handling exercises without support; this means the person should be capable of sitting upright without any additional anchoring required. The back thighs, hips and arms may be emphasized in the workout process. Squatting and leg- press exercises should be avoided if possible, although any cases where these exercises may be used should be monitored accordingly and with as little weight as possible, so as to prevent possible injuries.

Cancer Patients

Heavy lifting is not encouraged at the start of a workout routine. Limited lifting is needed due to the patient possibly experiencing fatigue due to cancer treatments or any surgical procedures. Chemotherapy or radiation processes may particularly influence the body's responses to workouts. Rest intervals may be expanded in length if needed.

Patients with Chronic Lung Illnesses

Those with cystic fibrosis or other chronic lung ailments can engage in lifting about 8 to 10 reps, with only one set, two to three days a week. Extra rest may be used in between each exercise to allow the person to recover. All progress should be managed gradually. Talk with a person to see if that he or she is ready to move on to the next step in the training process. Treadmill exercises are strongly encouraged. Such actions should be utilized with slow speeds and at a level slope. Leg pains should also be recognized.

Questions

1. The following point may be utilized as a part of the objective analysis of a patient:
    a. Analysis of occupation
    b. Dietary routines
    c. Weight and height
    d. Sleep habits

2. Free weights may be used in a workout routine, but this requires:
    a. Stability within the body
    b. An even amount of weight
    c. Proper handles on a free weight
    d. Changes in the body's temperature

3. Stabilization refers to:
    a. Supporting a certain range of motion
    b. Triggering proper connections in the nervous system
    c. Figuring out how to hold the weights
    d. All of the above

4. The goal of corrective flexibility exercises is to:
    a. Move the body back and forward quickly
    b. Keep certain positions for up to 30 seconds at a time
    c. Relieve pressure through physical rolling
    d. Allow for repeated motions

5. An autogenic inhibition exercise will help with managing an antagonist muscle for contractions. Meanwhile, the Golgi tendon organ, or GTO, will help with:
    a. Inhibiting contraction
    b. Promoting proper movements
    c. Shifting muscles
    d. Restoring natural functions

6. A multiple-set process involves:
    a. Using two or three sets of one exercise
    b. Handling many sets of multiple exercises
    c. Using different weights throughout the workout
    d. Working with two exercises quickly

7. Free weights are to be used during this part of the workout routine:
    a. Stabilization

b. Power
c. Strength
d. Preparation

8. Muscles that connect to the vertebrae in the spinal column help with:
    a. Stabilization
    b. Keeping the body strong
    c. Flexibility
    d. Endurance

9. Strength training exercises for balance purposes should include:
    a. Windmills
    b. Balances
    c. Balance and reach exercises
    d. Squats

10. Plyometric training focuses on the following points in a workout:
    a. Speed
    b. Strength
    c. Flexibility
    d. A and B

11. Proprioceptive plyometrics is different from regular plyometric training in that the proprioceptive format focuses on:
    a. Speed
    b. Coordination
    c. Balance
    d. Flexibility

12. A standing progression exercise will require significant changes in how well a workout routine is planned, based on:
    a. The footwear one uses in the workout process
    b. The amount of weight one is tasked to lift
    c. The stability of the surface
    d. Motions to handle

13. The most stable surface to use in a proprioceptive manipulation exercise is:
    a. Stability ball
    b. Foam pad
    c. Balancing disk
    d. Balance beam

14. The difference between quickness and agility in an SAQ training process involves:
    a. How much weight is applied to the body during the workout routine
    b. How quickly a person can change body position
    c. The timing in between reps or sets
    d. How fast one can move in general

15. Resisted sprints may only be planned in a workout routine when:
    a. The person is in an open environment
    b. The person has built the muscles necessary to handle the intense resistance
    c. The surface for running is flat and smooth
    d. All of the above

16. An undulating period for a workout design will entail varying workouts based on:
    a. The diversity of exercises
    b. How much weight is to be used
    c. The stage of one's workout
    d. How many reps or sets are to be used

17. A workout routine for an adult should be designed according to the FITTE principle, with this length standard at a time:
    a. 20 minutes
    b. 30 minutes
    c. 45 minutes
    d. 60 minutes

18. A risk vs. reward analysis for a design process should be utilized based on:
    a. Injury risk
    b. Types of exercises
    c. Speed of exercises
    d. B and C

19. A person is starting to develop added infections and is not performing as well as he or she used to. That person might not be getting enough sleep either. At this point, the person might be experiencing:
    a. Burnout
    b. Improper training
    c. Overtraining
    d. Possible muscle tears

20. The following equipment may be worn during a workout to improve upon reviewing how well the body is responding to a designed workout:
    a. Fitness band tracker
    b. Mobile tracking app
    c. Pedometer
    d. Heart-rate monitor

Answers

1. c. The weight and height are parts of an objective analysis that may be followed. This refers to data that a person can read and review.
2. a. A person who uses free weights will have to perform the movements in the workout in a proper line or with a clean motion.
3. d. The weights should be held accordingly in the stabilization process to improve upon how a person can handle a certain range of motion while allowing the nervous system to get used to what a person can handle.
4. b. An appropriate flexibility exercise can help with holding the body in position to improve upon how well the body can stay active.
5. a. Contractions around the muscle should be supported by the GTO. The opposite or antagonist muscle is not being worked upon, so it becomes easier for contractions to be handled accordingly.
6. b. A multiple-set effort focuses on handling multiple exercises that can include several sets for each. A single set concentrates on only one exercise, but this also involves working with many sets at a time. The pyramid set entails changing the weights that are handled in between sets.
7. c. Free weights help with building strength as they are to be used after a person has gotten used to some of the physical movements that are needed for one's success.
8. a. Stabilization is required for ensuring the body can handle more natural functions and complete them in as little time as possible.
9. d. The other exercises are designed with stabilization in mind. The squatting process strengthens the body.
10. d. The body has to be move faster, while also handling more stress, to ensure the body stays active during the lifting process.
11. c. A person must work towards identifying how certain movements are handled and how muscles can interact with each other during the proprioceptive training process. Part of this includes seeing how well the body responds to regular motions.

12. c. Standing progression moves from being on a stable surface to being on an unstable spot. Also, this goes from being on two legs to only being on one, regardless of the stability of the surface in question.
13. d. Although the balance beam itself is slim in width, the beam has a flat surface that will not shift around with use and therefore may be seen as the most stable surface.
14. b. Agility refers to being able to start and stop quickly. Quickness focuses on how much time it takes for a person's body position to change while still producing a high amount of power or force in the movement.
15. d. The environment one is in for the workout process should be as controlled and comfortable as possible. This includes seeing that the surface is open and that the area is not too hard to run on.
16. c. The undulating period may include cases where a person engages in either a stabilization, strength or power routine. The best process is to move in that order on alternating days.
17. b. The 30-minute standard in the FITTE principle is used to keep the patient from experiencing burnout.
18. a. A person's ability to handle a workout, based on the injuries he or she could experience, should be planned accordingly.
19. c. Overtraining occurs when the body works out far too much at one time.
20. d. A heart-rate monitor may help with identifying specific heart functions in the body and may be more accurate than what you would get out of a wrist-based tracker.

Domain 4: Exercise Technique and Training Instruction

Proper training is necessary for helping a patient to develop a healthier body, although the proper instruction is a necessity for ensuring that the patient can move forward in his or her work. The standards that must be used for a workout will vary based on the particular stage a person is in. The efforts involved can expand in intensity and effort, depending on the work that a person has to put in for getting a workout going.

Setting Up Exercises

Basic Process

The basic standard for setting up exercises involves the following steps:

1. Review the techniques and setups that are to be used for all the exercises one will enter into within a certain program.
2. Prepare a series of categories for each exercise. This includes a focus on stabilization, strength and power-based exercises.
3. Allow for regression at some point.
4. Review the terms for progression to allow a person to move forward and add more weights or physical efforts.
5. The patient starts performing the exercises that have been prescribed.

The process can work for all people who need assistance, especially for the three individual stages of exercise.

Flexibility

Flexibility exercises may be prepared with the following points for success:

Self-Myofascial Release

The self-myofascial release process entails the body being stretched on a roller or other item that a person's body may be applied to. The release is required to help stimulate more muscles and to prepare the body for physical activity. The SMR process may help with relieving tensions in many parts of the joints that are naturally difficult to work with. These areas are known mainly as trigger points. The training process for SMR should entail a few additional aspects:

1. The patient should target the tensions or trigger points around the joints while stretching. Part of this is to loosen tissues and to allow for blood to flow through an area.
2. Focus solely on the muscle tissues. The joints and bones should not be focused on, as doing so is not going to help the body recover.
3. The body must remain hydrated during the session. Water is especially required as an SMR session may result in added stress and pressure unless it is handled appropriately and safely.

When to Avoid SMR

SMR should be avoided when:

- The patient has varicose veins.
- The patient has hypertension that is not easy to control.
- The person has diabetes; this may be concerning if the patient has poor circulation in the legs due to diabetes.
- A woman is pregnant; SMR may be more dangerous in the first and third trimesters.
- When a person has an unclear or uncertain medical condition; proper medical clearance is required at this point.

A proper review of the patient's health and a general questionnaire surrounding his or her ability to handle exercises may be performed to get an idea of what a person is going through and what may be considered in terms of a workout plan.

Static

Static stretching may be planned when the patient needs to work on expanding the reaches of his or her muscles. This includes getting the muscles to stretch out to the point of tension, so they're triggered for an extended period. Static stretching may work for about 20 to 60 seconds before a regular workout routine begins. The timing may help with improving the patient's stabilization. Stretching for longer than two minutes may tax the muscles prematurely, thus causing a workout to be less effective.

When to Avoid Static Stretches

Do not utilize static stretches before a workout routine if:

- The patient is experiencing arthritis.

- A person has osteoporosis.
- The person has experienced an acute injury; this is especially concerning if that injury took place recently.

Active-Isolated

Active-isolated stretching may work in cases where the body is going to engage in shorter or faster actions. The activity may help with keeping the body strong. The practice is needed for cases where muscles might be tight or tense. The practice should work for less than a minute, if possible, to ensure the stretching process is controlled accordingly.

Dynamic Stretching

For dynamic stretching, reciprocal inhibition is required. The effort allows for a better of motion. The dynamic-stretching process can entail three to five movements, in one stretching position, to allow the body to loosen up and become ready to engage in certain activities. The stretching process works best in cases where the person is going to participate in activities that require fast and sudden motions.

Core

The core-training process can work with different points for each of the three stages of training:

1. Stabilization

A patient will use a stability ball or isometric hold for stabilization exercises. The exercises utilized must work for 12 to 20 reps, with one to four sets at a time. A slower tempo is needed to allow the patient to gently move through the required movements. Up to 90 seconds of rest is needed in between each set.

2. Strength

The core will have to move during strength-based exercises. About 8 to 12 reps should be used for exercises, with two or three sets involved for each routine. A medium tempo is required in this situation. About 60 seconds of rest may also be utilized at this point.

3. Power

Power exercises require the participant to throw items. Medicine balls or kettlebells may be used at this point for added control and support. Eight to 12 reps should be used for two to three sets at a time. The tempo can be at any rate that one wants it to be, although 60 seconds of rest is needed in between each set.

Balance

The progression part of balance training may start with an easy exercise and will eventually move on to something more complicated. Part of this includes looking at the stability needed for completing certain exercises. All of the body's planes of motion can be utilized during this part of training. However, the proprioception process requires working with the right amount of balance, based on how well a person is moving through the training process. The development of a workout plan should be as follows:

1. Stabilization

The exercises should not require any bending of the hip or leg that the body is planted on. A foam pad may also be utilized to add a bit of control, although that pad should not be unstable to the point where it might be difficult for a person to use. About 12 to 20 reps of light exercises may be conducted at a slow pace, with 90 seconds of rest in between each set.

2. Strength

The planted hip or knee can bend down at this point. Unilateral squats are among the more popular exercises that may be conducted at this juncture. About eight to 12 reps can be used at this point, with a moderate tempo. Sixty seconds can be used between each set for resting.

3. Power

Faster motions may be used, with hopping actions involved. The hopping should favor the planted leg. Eight to 12 reps are also needed with a moderate tempo. About 30 to 60 seconds are needed for rest in between sets.

Plyometric

Any planned plyometric exercises must be done with the intention of allowing the body to produce new forces. Any active forces around the body must be neutralized, with the movements being handled at a certain time.

1. Stabilization

The exercises at this point should be planned with a three- to five-second pause in between each landing. For instance, a person who partakes in a box-jump exercise must stay at the proper position on the box for a few seconds and then back in the original position for a few seconds after jumping back. The key is to allow the body to stabilize itself and to control how it responds to different situations and surfaces or stability levels. About five to eight reps will be fine for this stage in the exercise routine. The tempo should be consistent all the way through, if possible. Also, 90 seconds of rest is required in each session.

2. Strength

The repeated movements in strength exercises should be planned accordingly. Repeated jumps may be used, with about eight to 10 reps in a set. The tempo can be a little faster at this point, but it must still remain steady. About 60 seconds of rest will be needed after each set.

3. Power

The movements at this juncture should be as fast as possible. Power step-up exercises are popular in this case. About eight to 12 reps should be used in each set. The tempo can be at the participant's pace, but it is vital for that person to try to move quickly. About 60 seconds of rest may also be required at this point.

Speed, Agility and Quickness

The patient's stride rate and length should be noticed well at this point. The patient should attain distance in each stride while producing those strides as quickly as possible.

1. Stabilization

Sagittal plane movements are vital at the start. About two or three reps may be used at the start, with 60 seconds of rest in between each set. The patient only needs to complete one or two sets at a time.

2. Strength

Strength-based exercises focus mainly on frontal plane motions. Three to five reps are needed with three to four sets used at a time, plus 60 seconds of rest between sets.

3. Power

All planes of motion are to be utilized at this point. The most effort should be provided in these exercises. Three to five reps should be used with the same number of sets involved. Ninety seconds of rest should also be incorporated in the middle.

Resistance Training

Special parameters must be planned in the resistance training process, to allow the participant to receive the best possible results when looking to strengthen and tone muscle.

Cycle Length

For resistance training, one of three cycles may be utilized at this point:

1. Macrocycle – 6 to 12 months
2. Mesocycle – 3 to 4 months
3. Microcycle – Up to 1 month

A macrocycle is recommended for cases where a participant has a large amount of work to complete. The microcycle may be for short-term efforts, although several microcycles may be linked up together to produce one large macrocycle. This is recommended for cases where several stages have to be utilized in the workout process.

Movement Training

To start, a patient must learn how to handle the movements required for completing a workout the right way. Movement training entails two to three sessions of workouts in a week, with 10 to 20 reps for each exercise. A low level of intensity may be utilized at this juncture.

Endurance

Muscular endurance is the second part of resistance training. This is to focus on allowing the muscles to handle more weight at a time. At this point, a person needs three sessions each week, while using 12 to 16 reps in each set. The reps should be handled for about five to six seconds at a time. About two to three sets may be used at this point. About 60 seconds of rest may be used for each set. All regular movement patterns may be used at this point.

Strength

After the muscles are accustomed to the movements needed, the resistance training sessions can move on to strength-based efforts. About 72 hours should be spent in between each session for the best results. Around three to six reps of weight, at around 80 to 90 percent of the maximum that a person can handle, should be utilized for the best possible gains, but that total can go down to 70 percent for the earliest stages of training. About three or four sets should be good enough.

Power

Single-effort lifts may work with three to five sets, with one to two reps for each set. For multiple-effort lifts, three to five reps may work with the same number of sets. Up to 90 percent of the maximum weight total that a person can lift can be utilized at this point. The patient should also rest for about two to five minutes in between each set, to allow the body to recover from the heavy weights and the fast speeds involved with the practice.

Key Principles

- **Double-progressive.** In this part of the process, the number of reps that will be used should be increased regularly, with weights being added by five percent at each point.
- **Specificity.** The proper resistance and repetition periods should be used for each workout routine. Specific actions can be used in these workout points to allow the participant to have more control over his or her body.
- **Overload.** Overload refers to how a person has to train with a certain amount of weight throughout the workout process. A person should increase the weight of one's load by around five percent at a time to allow that person to handle more weight, although this must only be done when that participant is comfortable with the added weight and is ready to take on the extra effort involved.
- **Reversibility.** A person must be active in working out as there is a potential for any gains to be reversed if the person is not careful enough. The body loses its strength at about half the rate at which that strength was gained.
- **Diminishing returns.** As the body reaches its maximum strength, there is a need to change the workout around. The neuromuscular responses involved will become repetitive as the person has become far too used to certain motions. This makes it harder for the body to achieve new gains.

Adding Further Power

As the patient reaches a plateau, it may be best to adjust the lifting process and to plan new movements. Several solutions may be utilized to improve upon how well a person can develop further levels of power:

- **Plyometrics.** The movements used in plyometrics can work alongside the added muscle mass to produce more power within the body. This may help to maintain muscle mass and to improve upon the body's ability to stay active and functional.
- **Muscle-spindle contractions.** Added concentric contractions may be required to help improve upon how well the body can handle its motions.
- **Isometric-contraction control.** Such contractions must be avoided as they may cause added fatigue to the muscles. The patient's blood pressure may also increase if those contractions go on for a while.

Warm-Up Protocol

For warming up, the patient should engage in five to ten minutes of low-intensity movements that are not necessarily related to any of the motions that will be utilized during the following workout. Some specific warm-up routines may also be considered, as needed. These are actions that are like lighter versions of the movements one will partake in during the planned workout session. Gentle breathing exercises may be considered during the warm-up. The breathing is needed to help a participant to stay focused and prepared for the warm-up task at hand. Warm-ups are designed with multiple intentions:

- A warm-up may increase the patient's heart rate, thus making it easier for that patient to stay active during a workout.
- The cardiovascular system's capacity to keep working will improve.
- Blood flow will increase around the active area of the body that the patient will be working on.
- The temperature of the tissue being supported will increase.
- Muscle contractions will be easier for the body to support.
- The body's metabolic rate may also increase.

Types of Exercises

The exercises a person may partake in during the warm-up process can vary, but the following may help with improving how well the body is prepared for the activity:

- Hip rotations
- Reverse lunges
- Rope jumping; this works best when done at a slower pace
- Squats
- Sit-ups or push-ups, among other forms of calisthenics
- Basic static stretches

The key is to focus on movements that involve the muscles or other body parts that will be worked upon. A foam roller may also be applied along tissues around the body to release any possible tensions.

Cool-Down Protocol

The cool-down process requires the person to move back into a state of rest. This requires the person to engage in lighter activities after the intense workout or lifting is complete. Cool-down exercises that may be utilized include the following:

- **Light cardiovascular activities.** This may work for about five to ten minutes at a time. A slight jog or gentle walk may be appropriate for allowing the body to relax.

- **Static stretching.** While the stretches may be held for up to 30 seconds at a time, those stretches are needed for helping the body to feel stimulated and to keep cramps from developing in certain tissues.

- **SMR.** This process works best for cases where a person has worked on a certain part of the body for much longer than others, and extra maintenance is therefore needed on that part to keep it healthy or active.

Failure to follow a cool-down protocol may result in intense pain. The cool-down period may last for about five to ten minutes. The key is to allow the body to feel rested after the process is finished.

Kinesthetic, Auditory and Visual Cueing Techniques

The following techniques focus on producing feedback. The feedback entails sensory information that promotes healthy motor patterns. The feedback used can be found in two forms, with each being different based on what a person can engage in:

1. External

External feedback focuses on sensory information that is produced by an outside source. You may produce this feedback, although this may also come from a fitness tracker or app or from a mirror that the patient looks into. The external feedback utilized will give the participant feedback on his or her performance and how well results have been attained during an activity. This can be noticed from changes in the body, from what you identify in the person or from what the fitness program reports.

2. Internal

Internal feedback focuses on sensory information. This includes anything that may identify how well an environment is being managed. A general feedback process may help with identifying some of the actions that a person is participating in when aiming to be healthy.

Kinesthetic

Kinesthetic cueing involves helping a person to do something and to think about how that action feels. In most cases, this entails helping that person complete a workout. The practice focuses on touching and moving. A person will not concentrate on the workout routine if that someone is not stimulated accordingly. It is through regular actions that a person will stay fit and healthy during the workout routine.

The kinesthetic training process can entail the following cues:

- Some handheld toys may be provided to give a person something to do with his or her hands. A soft ball, or something like Play-Doh, may be used to maintain a sense of stimulation while also preparing the hands for any lifting actions that may take place.
- Some fragrances or scents may be added to a workout environment to ease the mind. This should be used for creating a pleasing environment for a workout routine, but scents should not be overwhelming.
- Breaks may be taken during the workout routine for stretching.
- Music can be played during a workout, if necessary, or if it is appropriate for that person.

Auditory

Auditory cueing involves telling a person how to do an exercise. This may also involve having the participant talk with the trainer about what he or she is doing and anything they may think or feel during the workout process.

Some of the auditory actions that may be utilized include:

- Explaining what is coming up next in the workout.
- Summarizing any actions performed.
- The Socratic method of discussing points with the participant can be utilized. You can get as much information from that person as possible and then find ways to fill in any gaps or to figure out how certain uncertainties that a person has may be resolved. The key to this method is to let the participant figure out what can be done to improve upon his or her own individual work situation.
- Allowing a person to verbalize the instructions. This may assist that person in fully understanding how certain routines are to be followed.

The auditory information may help a person to recall the information and to keep it in mind throughout the entire workout process. This does exceptionally well in cases where the content being handled is detailed.

Visual

Visual cueing involves showing a person how to complete certain physical actions. The practice may work with spatial and linguistic functions. A spatial learner will do well with charts, written words and videos that illustrate the things one can do in a workout. A linguistic learner will write down the things that he or she is hearing when being instructed. Actions to consider for visual learning include:

- The use of graphics and charts will help people to identify some of the fitness goals that they need to attain.
- Videos or illustrations of certain actions may be utilized.
- Any handouts that are to be provided to a person when learning about certain actions should have some white space for a person to write on.
- A person may be asked to review the topic verbally. This is to recap whatever he or she is entering into during the workout process. The visual sensations that a person gets out of the workout should be analyzed accordingly.

Regardless of the form of cueing that is used, the focus is to be careful with one's mental processes and to think about the positive actions that may take place. The goal is to ensure that the person is active and ready to continue working out for the long term.

Safety Considerations

When managing a patient or participant, it is critical to ensure that person is supported in a secure and safe environment or atmosphere. Safety considerations include the following:

- Figure out the exercises that are appropriate for a client to participate in. The exercises should be relevant to the specific fitness needs that someone has.
- Look at any contraindications in the exercise process. These include situations where certain exercises may not be effective or could actually put a person at risk of harm.
- Assess how intense the exercises are. The exercises should be intense enough for a person to participate in, but should not be rough to the point where they increase the likelihood of injury.

- The number of exercises that a person can utilize, and the number of reps or sets of each that a person can handle, must be analyzed. A person should only be allowed to do a certain number that he or she is capable of physically capable of handling without the risk of fatigue or injury.
- The number of workout sessions a person can handle should also be noticed. Some people may be able to work out four or five days in a week, but others might be at risk of harm from overexertion.

Environmental Considerations

The environment that a person where a person works out should be planned accordingly. There are several aspects that may be considered when getting a workout up and running:

- **Ventilation.** Enough ventilation must be provided in a workout environment to ensure air moves through well enough to keep a person from overheating and becoming fatigued quickly.
- **Open space.** A person needs to have enough space for a workout to make it easy for that person to move about with a full range of motion.
- **Number of people.** A person should not be surrounded by too many people during the workout routine. This is to ensure the person will not be too fixated on others in the workout process.
- **Lighting.** Enough lighting is required in a workout environment to ensure a person can easily see where he or she is moving.

Exercise Intensity Monitoring

Be aware of the following points:

- Review all cases where a person's breathing becomes heavier or more intense. You may have to stop the workout at this point.
- Look at the effort a person puts into attempting to lift weights or engage in certain functions. A fatigued person will develop significant injury concerns and may operate slowly.
- Cases, where a person is unable to manage certain motions or movements in a set, are signs that a workout is too intense.
- Any instances where the body's range of motion changes or there are changes in the way the body shifts should be noticed.

Equipment Setup Effort

All equipment used in the workout process should be reviewed for effectiveness:

- Review the cables around any machines being used to see that the machine is aligned so the grip produced is effective.
- Check the handles for any equipment that may be used. The handles should be strong enough to support most lifting functions without possibly binding or becoming slip hazards.
- Look at how the weights are represented on your equipment. The weights should be planned out to give you extra control over the efforts needed for a proper workout.
- Any flooring surfaces that the equipment will be situated on should be examined carefully to ensure there are no hazards that might cause slipping or undue difficulty.

Spotting Points

The spotting process requires:

1. A review of the plans that someone has for lifting weights.

The plans should be organized based on how many reps and sets will be used. This should be planned based on the general effort one plans on putting into the workout.

2. Being aware of how well a person is lifting the weights.

Watch for how a person is handling weights and ensure that the person is not struggling with them. You should not take a weight from a lifter unless that person is at risk of losing control.

3. Allowing for some assistance in monitoring the person's lifting efforts, but being sure you're allowing that person to go through the natural process of lifting.

Having a hands-off approach for lifting helps, as you allow a person to handle a full range of motion throughout the entire process. This works best when that person is capable of managing the load accordingly and without stress.

4. Always spotting at the wrists.

Do not spot at the elbows. Observe the wrists when a person is lifting, to see that the person is capable of handling the weights without struggles. Observing at the elbows only delves into a small portion of the body at this juncture.

5. Keeping your hands away from a weight stack while spotting.

This fifth point is particularly vital for when you are helping a patient with a machine-based exercise routine. The hands should not be near a weight stack, as the weights might fall apart depending on how much effort is put into the workout effort. This could be a risk due to the intensity of the weights involved with the lifting process.

Unusual Breathing Patterns

Any cases where a person develops unusual breathing patterns during a workout should be carefully identified. The key at this point is to identify when a person's breathing changes and whether certain things have to be done to resolve the breathing issues.

1. Shallow Breathing

Shallow breathing occurs as muscles other than the diaphragm are being used for respiratory functions.

2. Excess Breathing

Excess breathing may be observed from a person taking in more breaths than what one might regularly put in during a workout. These excess breaths can be harmful as they may cause dizziness and headaches. Such breaths can also be intense to where a person will become lightheaded and unable to complete a workout within a suitable amount of time.

3. Lack of Oxygen

A person who struggles with significant breathing concerns may develop a lack of oxygen. This occurs as a person's oxygen levels in the blood falls. The metabolic waste produced during the workout increases in intensity, thus resulting in fatigue throughout the muscles. Stiffness may also develop. Encourage participants to work with natural breathing motions to improve upon their ability to keep a healthy workout moving. This includes taking rest periods between sets and managing the proper breathing motions throughout the entire process. The goal is to ensure that the person is not irritated and feels confident in his or her ability to manage a workout the right way.

Kinetic Chain Checkpoints

Checkpoints are required for identifying possible dysfunctions throughout the body. Corrective measures must be utilized in cases where a person struggles to handle proper functions.

Ankles

The ankle must point straight ahead. The patient must land on the heel. Pronation and supination must be avoided, if possible, during the running process.

Knees

The knee must be properly aligned with the second and third toes. Abduction and adduction must be avoided.

Lumbo-Pelvic-Hip Complex

The hips need to be in a neutral position as the patient's fastest possible speed is attained. The low back should be controlled well, with a minimal amount of arching.

Shoulders

The shoulders should be straight and at an even height when compared with one another during the workout. Cases where the shoulders are not handled appropriately may cause the tissues to wear out and develop premature fatigue due to the weak movements involved. The rotator cuff may handle some of the compression-based actions and functions in the workout process, although this is based on the person's comfort.

Head

The head has to be kept straight ahead during a workout. The head should not be positioned forward by much. The patient may keep his or her head down on occasion, to review how the body is moving at the start. This should be avoided as the patient gets used to the exercises. This is to allow the person to focus on what is ahead and to ensure the body can create the proper connections for a workout.

Physical or Medical Signs That Suggest Changes Are Needed to a Training Routine

After a while, a person may require certain changes in a workout routine. There are a few things to consider when looking at when a person needs to make changes in a training routine:

1. A person is having a very easy time with managing the lifting efforts.

Eventually, a person may be able to easily lift weights to the point where he or she might no longer feel very stimulated or challenged during the workout process. You may consider looking for other workout routines, or even add more weight to the lifting process; the latter idea should only work when a person feels comfortable with handling those weights.

2. The heart rate is too low.

A person who has a low heart rate during the workout process might need to use different exercises and routines to improve the overall effect of the workout. A person who has a low heart rate will not receive enough support for building muscle mass or burning off fat. Therefore, new strategies may be utilized in the workout routine to increase heart rate and ensure the rate increases over time.

3. A person is not experiencing any positive changes.

Sometimes a person might need a change in a workout as a means of improving upon how the body responds to the efforts being put in. You have to review how well a person's body is developing and whether someone is moving forward steadily. The key is to ensure there are no struggles that might come along in the effort involved with trying to stay healthy and active. You may talk with a person who is trying to complete a workout and ask about anything they think would help develop a better routine.

Questions

1. Which categories should be used when planning the exercises one will utilize in a workout routine?
    a. Strength
    b. Power
    c. Stabilization
    d. All of the above

2. Regression is to be allowed at some point in the workout process. This refers to:
    a. Adding extra time in between sets
    b. Fixing the technique based on movements
    c. A person moving backward in the workout process
    d. Stopping the workout routine

3. What should be done if you are uncertain if a person can handle an SMR technique?
    a. Ask if that person is comfortable with the technique
    b. Assess the person's body
    c. Ask that person's medical professional
    d. Hold off altogether

4. What should be done for stretching if a person has arthritis?
    a. Keep working for two minutes
    b. Stretch for about 20 seconds
    c. Avoid stretching altogether
    d. Ask the patient if he or she is comfortable with the movement

5. When should a medicine ball be used in the training process?
    a. During the power stage
    b. At the start
    c. When building muscle mass
    d. Only when desired

6. Any hopping motions used for balance-based exercises should include:
    a. The body favoring the planted leg
    b. The hopping being done as quickly as possible
    c. About 90 seconds of rest between sets
    d. Avoiding resistance

7. Plyometric exercises should include a brief pause in between each rep during the stabilization process. The pause between reps should last for:
    a. 1 second
    b. 2 seconds
    c. 5 seconds
    d. 10 seconds

8. During the power stage of a plyometric technique, the tempo should be:
    a. As fast as possible
    b. Generally controlled
    c. At the user's pace
    d. Moderate

9. Frontal plane motions are needed for an SAQ process during this stage:
    a. Stabilization
    b. Strength
    c. Power
    d. None

10. A macrocycle can last for:
    a. 1 month
    b. 4 months
    c. 6 months
    d. 10 months

11. Can a macrocycle be made up of several microcycles when planning a technique process?
    a. Yes
    b. No
    c. Only a few
    d. Based on the user's discretion

12. A seated military press can be planned in a stabilization process, but the proper technique for this should entail the following:
    a. Lying on one's back during this motion
    b. Keeping the tempo as fast as possible
    c. Using a ball for balancing
    d. Adding extra rest after each set

13. Barbell lifts can work when this technique is used for the training process:
    a. A jerk and clean effort is needed

b. Extra weight for overloading is required
c. The motions must be fast
d. A person can handle up to 20 reps at a time

14. Can basic stabilization or strength exercises be used in a power technique?
    a. Yes
    b. No
    c. Based on the person's need
    d. When a doctor recommends this

15. A double-progressive technique entails the number of reps being increased while the weight is increased at each set by this many percentage points:
    a. 5
    b. 10
    c. 15
    d. 20

16. When the muscles stop responding well, a person will develop:
    a. Burnout
    b. Diminishing returns
    c. Reversibility
    d. Added fatigue

17. A warm-up routine can last for:
    a. 2 minutes
    b. 3 minutes
    c. 7 minutes
    d. 15 minutes

18. SMR works during the cool-down period in cases where:
    a. A part of the body was worked on more than others
    b. Tension is felt in one part
    c. A person has worn out a joint
    d. The process should actually be avoided

19. Internal feedback concentrates mainly on:
    a. What a CPT says to a participant
    b. Looking into a mirror
    c. Reviewing a fitness tracker
    d. Sensory information

20. Handheld stimulation may be used for the following:
    a. To stimulate the body
    b. To become alert
    c. To prepare for handling weights
    d. For pleasure

Answers

1. d. The three categories are the basics to use when planning a workout technique the right way.
2. c. Regression may work in cases where a person is struggling with trying to manage certain loads or has gone through more pressure or stress in the workout than what one can regularly afford to manage.
3. c. A medical professional can be contacted to see if that person can be cleared for a certain exercise routine
4. c. Arthritis patients should not be forced into stretching motions that they might not be overly comfortable with handling. These actions may trigger more irritation in a person's joints.
5. a. Medicine balls, kettle bells and other weights that may be tossed around may be used in the power stage.
6. a. Resistance can be added if desired. The tempo should be moderate. Other than that, the body must support the weight off of the leg that person wishes to favor.
7. c. The five-second time period is useful for planning general efforts for managing a person's balance and keeping that balance from being too difficult to handle.
8. a. All movements must be managed quickly and without struggles.
9. b. After the sagittal plane movements in the stabilization effort, the strength process will require frontal plane motions. After that, all planes of motion may be utilized during the power process.
10. d. Although a macrocycle can be six months in length at the least, it is best to keep that cycle close to a year in length, if possible.
11. a. The microcycles can be planned to mix into one large macrocycle if the workout technique one wishes to use has an extended series of stages that target multiple objectives or values.
12. c. The participant can sit on a ball to allow for a bit of balance. The ball should be settled on a flat surface where it will not be at risk of slipping or otherwise being too hard to use.
13. a. The jerk and clean process will help with identifying the way the body can handle motions and move forward without a struggle.
14. a. Exercises from the first parts of the workout process may be used in a power technique, provided that the weights being used are a little lighter in intensity.

The lightweight effort is to allow for extra weight to be pressed and handled accordingly.

15. a. A smaller percentage total may be utilized, but five percent is the optimal choice here.
16. b. Diminishing returns occur as the body gets used to a weight to the point where the muscle response is not all that strong. Burnout will focus mainly on mental and emotional fatigue.
17. c. Try to keep the warm-up process going for about five to 10 minutes. The timing should be consistent with what works after the workout is finished within the cool-down effort.
18. a. The excessive pressure that comes from the body should be noticed accordingly. A person who put in a large amount of effort on one part should have the area relaxed, although this will only work if the person's body is not at risk of any harm.
19. d. A person's senses are responsible for managing internal processes. Such senses may involve cases where a person experiences pain or irritation.
20. c. Whether it entails Play-Doh or another flexible item for the hands to play with, the kinetic stimulation will help the hands become flexible and ready for a workout. This is mainly for cases where someone has to lift heavy items.

Domain 5: Client Relations and Behavioral Coaching

It is vital for a CPT to properly support a client. You will have to work on improving upon how well a client functions and how motivated that client is to continue working out and putting forth a strong effort.

Motivational Points

It is vital for a participant in a fitness program to feel motivated and encouraged to continue working towards managing a healthy routine. Motivation relating to exercises focuses on many key points for helping the body to stay active and functional.

Intrinsic vs. Extrinsic

Intrinsic motivation: A person will enjoy the exercise and the emotions that come with it. Those who are intrinsically motivated will have an increased desire to continue working out.

Extrinsic motivation: Extrinsic motivation involves a person participating in exercises for reasons outside of pleasure. This may be for weight loss or for building muscle mass. Sometimes this may also be for helping to establish new relationships with other people.

Self-Efficacy

Self-efficacy is a measure of a person's desire to continue to work towards a healthy routine. A person who feels capable of completing the required exercises or motions in a routine will feel encouraged and active in his or her efforts.

Maintaining Motivation

It is vital to help a person feel encouraged and active in a workout by keeping that person motivated. Various ideas may be used to help with encouraging a sense of motivation.

1. Find someone who can work as a workout partner.

A person who is working with another individual, whether it is you or another person in a similar program, will feel encouraged to continue to work towards completing a program the right way.

2. Find exercises or activities that a person might enjoy.

A person needs to be focused on activities that he or she looks forward to. These include activities where a person is capable of staying functional and willing to exercise right.

3. Be assertive.

A sense of assertiveness should be encouraged among all people in a workout session. People must be honest and direct with each other when it comes to reviewing workouts and how they are progressing.

4. Provide appropriate coping strategies for helping people to manage any of the issues they come across.

Part of this includes working with stress and time-management efforts. This will be covered in further detail later in this guide.

Managing Proper Communication with Your Client

You must be capable of communicating well with your client in order for all persons involved to feel comfortable and confident. This establishes the ground for a great workout routine.

Rapport Building

Rapport building involves creating a sense of support that builds over time and creates a positive impression on people.

When building rapport with a participant:

1. Keep your voice strong, without sounding weak or too firm.
2. Produce direct eye contact without looking intimidating.
3. Create a genuine emotion in your facial expression. Avoid trying to create a false impression.
4. Hand gestures may be used, but avoid having too many as that might be distracting.
5. Maintain a good posture that shows how confident you are in your work.

A sense of rapport is required to not only create a good relationship but also to get a person to feel motivated in the process of working out. Part of this includes ensuring there are no struggles involved with trying to move forward and getting a workout running to a person's general liking.

Added Steps for Building Rapport

The following steps may be used alongside the key points for establishing rapport:

1. Review behaviors and consider how well that person is capable of changing said behaviors or actions.

2. Plan a series of goals that someone can attain and utilize. Having a realistic series of goals for a person may help with establishing a better connection as you are showing that you understand what they are capable of doing.

3. Demonstrate and instruct a patient in what he or she should be doing in a workout routine. The goal is to let that person feel more comfortable with what is being taught in a workout session.

4. Be open with the person about how well the workout routine is moving and whether there are any problems that might be noticed in the workout routine. The work involved must be planned based on what someone feels is right and easy to work with.

Showing Empathy

Empathy is a display of your understanding of what someone else is thinking. With empathy, you are showing that you recognize the needs and concerns that someone might have. You are focusing on what is meaningful to a person, without going over the unnecessary details. For empathy, you have to recognize the emotional patterns that a person is exhibiting. Be aware of any differences between yourself and the other person when communicating. Recognize how you can adapt to the differences that someone is conveying.

Validating Activities and Actions

Any actions that someone enters into should be reviewed based on what that person is doing and how well that participant can handle certain actions. Talk with a person to identify what that someone might be thinking about a workout routine. As what is working, what isn't and discuss what can be done to resolve any concerns.

Communication Techniques

Verbal

Verbal communication may be measured with a series of steps:

1. A speaker says something.

2. The listener pays attention to what that speaker says.

3. The listener attaches a meaning to what that speaker is saying. This may match up with whatever the speaker really meant, although this is not the case every time.

For the best results, you must do the following:

- Directly explain to the client what it is you want.

Talk about any policies or procedures you wish to utilize, as well as any expectations that you have for a person to follow when aiming to complete a task.

- Be willing to express positive feelings and words of encouragement.

Show that you understand the person's emotional needs.

- Always be open to a person when you first meet them.

Part of this includes greeting someone with a positive tone and a smile.

- Be ready to go into more detail or to explain things in further detail, if necessary.

Nonverbal

Nonverbal communication requires extra effort. When it comes to things that cannot be communicated with simple words:

- Always offer a smile and other positive forms of body language to someone when greeting that person for the first part of the session.
- Show an active body when expressing things, but avoid trying to be too rough or otherwise hard to talk with.
- Show that you understand the many changes that a person is going through in a workout. Look for nonverbal cues like when a person is not as active as he or she was at the start of a workout. This is to help the person feel an added sense of control for the workout and what he or she wishes to do with it.

Nonverbal cues may require multiple sessions and uses for them to work accordingly. The effort must be planned based on what a person feels is right and how well an effort may move forward.

Listening to the Patient

The patient's needs should be observed. Part of this includes listening to what someone has to say. Two forms of listening are to be utilized:

Active Listening

Active listening involves paying attention to what the client is thinking. This includes analyzing the feelings that someone has and what that person wants to do with a workout routine. You must be aware of what a person is saying based on the following:

- The tone or rate at which a person is speaking
- Any particular words or feelings that a person is attempting to convey in the process
- Any attitudes that someone has based on the workout being supported

Paraphrasing (reflecting)

Paraphrasing or reflecting is required in cases where you are trying to discern what a person feels. This may help with confirming that you are paying attention to someone and that you recognize that person's needs. The effort will show that you respect the participant. In short, this involves reflection. Paraphrasing may entail repeating the same point a person is saying but in a shorter form. The key is to express a sense of understanding while also confirming that someone does feel a certain way or is putting in a certain form of activity in the process of working.

Asking Questions

You must ask questions of your participant in order to get a clear idea of what he or she is doing or to plan the right workout for the future.

Open-Ended

Open-ended questions are nondirective questions that allow a person to answer in any way one sees fit. The intention is to glean as much information as possible from someone. The information may include facts relating to what someone is trying to do for success and to maintain a healthy routine in the process.

Closed-Ended

A closed-ended question is a directive question that entails a yes or no answer. This may also include other answers, but this would be for cases where extremely specific variables are to be included.

Goal Analysis

Goals may be produced to help with giving the participant a purpose for wanting to workout and become healthy. Goals are divided up into short and long-term objectives. The short-term ones and require smaller efforts, while long-term points involve putting in extra effort to get the best results in the end.

Analyzing the Client's Expectations

The client's expectations should be investigated in detail. The person must be asked about what he or she wants to do in the long and short term. The person must want to achieve certain things while also having reasons.

SMART Goals

The SMART system for analyzing a client's goals should be utilized accordingly. This five-part approach reviews what a person wishes to do in the workout process, alongside the basic efforts he or she is willing to put into the process.

1. Specific

First, the goals that a person has must be specific. There must be an outcome that is clearly defined and which can be realistically attained if enough work is put in.

2. Measurable

There must be some kind of measure that exists with a goal. It will be difficult for a client to manage the goal if the results cannot be measured.

3. Attainable

The goal should be something that a person can reasonably attain if enough effort is put into the process. The work may be challenging, but it should not be intense enough to the point where a person will struggle to succeed.

4. Realistic

The client should be willing to go forward with the goal. The goal should be something that can be reached within a sensible time period, provided that person is willing to put in a conscious effort to make it happen.

5. Timely

The person must also have a time frame for when a goal is to be attained. The date can be very specific, but it must be realistic.

Discussing Reasonable Expectations

The SMART system may be used for analyzing the goals that a person has. You can talk with a person about those goals when you have identified certain concerns relating to the SMART system and how someone is planning on reaching those goals. The participant should verbalize his or her goals. The verbalization process helps to confirm the feelings or attitudes that someone has about a goal. The intention is to confirm that someone is ready to complete a specific task and that the person feels that the goal being set is realistic and should not be hard to attain if enough of an effort is put into the process. Be sure to also discuss what a person can expect to enjoy during a workout process:

- The client should have everything he or she needs for beginning an exercise or training routine. A person who has further questions should ask them in order to get proper clarification.
- The general clientele of a workout facility or program can be consulted. The key is to let someone fit in well with the others who are working on similar fitness goals.
- The clothing that may be worn during a workout should be discussed in detail. The patient should be comfortable but should still adhere to proper rules for training.
- Social facilitation may be discussed regarding how well a person may interact with others who are aiming to exercise. A discussion on what to expect out of one's behavior and ability to exercise may be held to confirm a person's ability to stay fit and productive.

Identifying Relevant Outcomes

The goals can be discussed in the next step. You can choose to revisit goals later on and figure out if those goals should be changed around later on. Such a plan helps with recognizing any concerns that someone might have and whether things need to change in any situation. Again, any goals that are to be planned in this case should be relevant to your goals and a demand to move forward. Be sure to see how the goals can be planned based on the desires you have for helping someone while being smart and easy to follow.

Supporting Lifestyle and Behavioral Changes

You must support the changes that a person expresses a desire for in a workout, in order to improve upon how well that participant will adhere to certain routines. A patient's confidence may increase over time, thus resulting in that person being willing to adhere to a routine and to move forward with the process involved.

Education

A person may be likely to continue to move forward in a fitness program when that person is educated about the process. This includes a full explanation of all the activities a person will be partaking in and how well the body is responding to those actions. A person who recognizes what is going on in the workout process may feel more motivated. This includes being able to notice any things that may be taking place in a routine and the need to make the appropriate changes based on what a person feels is right.

Monitoring Functions

A person may be monitored regularly during the workout process to see how well he or she is capable of handling certain exercises. Review how well a person is completing exercises and routines based on any changes in behavior or how that someone is responding to certain actions in the workout process.

Communication Strategies

For the best possible chances at improving upon your communication with someone:

- Show an understanding of a person's culture. This includes showing that you recognize the values that a person holds.
- Express empathy throughout the workout process and continue to build rapport.
- Show a professional attitude in your work. The feeling shows that you understand the needs that someone has for completing a workout the right way.

You can talk with a person in any form, but it is vital to show that you recognize that person's attitudes and feelings. Your client will feel more confident in what you are offering and will feel that you recognize his or her concerns.

Coping With and Managing Barriers to Proper Change

Many people who want to attain healthier bodies will come across significant boundaries that will keep them from moving forward in their efforts. The following section focuses on those barriers and struggles, alongside what can be done to control such concerns.

Stress Management

Stresses in life may be a factor for keeping a person from being able to handle exercises and motions the right way. Part of the work involved in managing one's physical efforts includes a few points of note:

- A person may be encouraged to work with gentle breathing motions and actions when aiming to rest and restore the body.
- Yoga can be encouraged among people who are looking to feel comfortable before or after a workout. You may refer a client to a yoga practitioner for help.

- Walking may be encouraged before or after a workout. Walking helps a person to relax the mind and body and can work well for when a person is trying to wind down after an exercise routine.

- Pilates is also encouraged for helping people to relieve stresses and to tone their muscles. You may refer a client to a Pilates expert or practitioner for help with certain functions.

Time Management

A patient may feel as though he or she does not have enough time to complete certain tasks or routines. The actions that may be supported in a time-management routine include:

- Set limits as to how long a person might work with certain people. This includes producing limits on how often a person is around others who might create a negative influence on a workout routine.

- Review how well a workout routine can be planned alongside a person's lifestyle. This includes planning a routine alongside any work obligations that an individual might have and any other personal needs.

- Analyze the types of workout routines and exercises a person is performing. You might have to plan new workouts based on what is most effective and efficient based on the work someone puts into a routine. The key is to make the most out of the time that someone has for getting a workout effort running.

A person may be consulted regarding the timing of a routine and any outside concerns one has when trying to organize the program. Time management makes it easier for someone to develop a stronger routine for working out accordingly.

Interpersonal Influences

Interpersonal concerns may be troubling as they relate to feelings that a person has about his or her efforts to become healthy and to complete a workout routine. The following points may be used to help with organizing a participant's interpersonal influences and keeping them from being difficult for a person to follow:

- Have a person take a look at the goals that he or she might have.

- Ask that person about the workout routines that he or she is entering into. There might be a need to change that person's efforts around and to incorporate different workout plans.

- Review how well that person is handling exercise routines. Sometimes a person's efforts might change based on any perceptions that he or she comes across when trying to complete a successful workout.

External Influences

External influences relate to outside concerns in a person's life that might make it harder for someone to succeed in a workout routine. Some of the external concerns may relate to family-related events and workplace activities. Sometimes these points may cause stresses in a person's life. You may talk with your client by asking about that person's work and family life and see if there are any noticeable concerns that might be causing the individual to forget about physical workout routines and efforts. You may discuss plans for managing new workout routines, if necessary. Be sure to talk with a person, but do not get to where you might be prying too deeply into a person's life and work efforts. You need to show restraint while also figuring out whether you need to adjust a person's work routine. It may also be best to have a person talk with a psychologist to figure out concerns and issues relating to external influences. Part of this includes looking at what can be done to produce coping mechanisms for handling problems.

Models of Behavior in Fitness

A patient's behavior may change during a fitness routine. These changes may occur as a person finds certain ideas for what he or she can do when aiming to manage a proper workout routine.

Health Belief Model

The health belief model focuses on how a person will want to keep working to improve his or her workout or dietary routine based on the fear of health-related issues. A person may focus on workouts based on the perceived seriousness of a concern. In this case, a person will feel more likely to engage in workout routines if that person feels that the significance of a medical issue is greater. This can particularly be noticed in those who have family histories that entail medical problems.

A person's perceived susceptibility may also be a factor. Susceptibility is a person's feeling about the chances of developing a significant health threat. Certain cues to action may also develop in this model. The cues involve things that people can do when trying to move forward and keep active.

Self-Efficacy Model

The self-efficacy model involves a person's perception of whether he or she can succeed.

The expectations that a person has over his or her ability to succeed are based on:

- Prior workout performances
- Any experiences someone had in workouts in the past
- The feedback that someone receives; this is regardless of whether it is positive or negative
- Vicarious experiences where a person sees someone else engage in certain actions
- A person's emotional state surrounding a workout
- Anything that person imagines may happen during a workout routine
- The patient's physiological state

Transtheoretical Model

The transtheoretical model concentrates on how well a person is ready to make a change. A participant has to be prepared to make changes to workout efforts and routines in order to succeed and move forward.

The Stages of Change

The transtheoretical model focuses on a pattern that a person may partake in when aiming to handle a workout routine. There are five stages that may develop in a fitness program based on a person's behaviors:

1. Precontemplation; finding a reason to work out

A person at this point is not someone who is actively working out. That someone might not have an intention to start working out within the next six months.

2. Contemplation; actually considering what to do in the workout

At this point, the person should consider getting into a routine within the next six months. You must listen to what that person needs and figure out a way to plan a workout routine based on those specific concerns that are being expressed.

3. Preparation; getting ready to act upon what was contemplated

There should not be specific routines at this point. The SMART goal system may be used to figure out what a person can do.

4. Action; performing what a person has prepared for

This is only for the start of the workout process. Proper education must be provided to the person to allow him or her to understand what is being managed in the workout effort.

5. Maintenance; continuing to keep a routine moving while using the same planned actions

The workout routine at this point should have gone on for at least the last six months. However, a person may still be tempted by prior habits; therefore, that person should continue to put in a consistent effort for working out. A person who goes through these stages will make progress. Those who go backwards will encounter a relapse as the workout in question becomes less effective and successful.

What Causes People to Change Their Behaviors

A person's actions must be observed carefully during the training process. The goal of your work is to ensure that a person is ready to engage in the proper behaviors and to move forward with a good routine for working out accordingly.

Operant Conditioning

A person may change behaviors in a workout routine based on the principles of operant conditioning. In this, a person's actions are influenced by the consequences that he or she observes or cases where certain people are impacted by various actions. An antecedent will be produced in the operant conditioning process. This stimulus will come before a behavior and will produce feelings that certain consequences are to develop. Antecedents may also be controlled in an attempt to try and make people participate in certain positive actions. For instance, a person might set the alarm earlier than usual to try and avoid possibly being late to a workout appointment. The consequences that are perceived in the process may influence a person in many forms:

- Positive reinforcement develops when a person feels that certain actions will increase the potential for certain behaviors to develop.
- Negative reinforcement prompts a person to remove stimuli that may cause negative results or avoid events that may trigger bad things.
- Punishments may be produced when a person participates in negative events. The punishment will aim to reduce the potential for a person to engage in a certain behavior once again in the future.

While punishments may help with controlling behaviors, these should not be used often as they may cause a person to become fearful and may keep that person from enjoying certain activities.

- Extinction develops as a positive stimulus that comes after a behavior is removed. The effort is made to reduce the potential for that behavior to occur once again.

Extinction is for cases where a person is to be trained away from a certain kind of behavior.

Shaping

Shaping develops as a skill is taught to someone in a gradual manner. The demands of the participant are light at the start, but they will become more intense as the workout process moves forward. The process works for managing self-efficacy and allows the participant to feel confident. The shaping process should be done to where the person can follow along without being difficult to the point where a person might become frustrated with the efforts involved.

Observational Learning

People may observe what others are doing to identify cases where they are not doing things the right way during their exercise routines. Observational learning helps people to recognize when they need to change their behaviors and move on to different kinds of actions. Observational learning works best when a person is in an environment with fewer people. This includes cases where you are the only one that is instructing a person on how to do things.

Stimulus Control

Stimulus control occurs when you make adjustments to an environment in the hopes of changing someone's actions. Part of this is to change possible actions and to improve upon a person's willpower. The effort may help with reducing any possible problems that someone might encounter during a workout routine.

Modifying Behaviors

Multiple strategies may be used when aiming to modify behaviors to improve upon a person's ability to complete a workout routine the right way:

1. Keep the training session at a sensible difficulty.

Avoid anything that may be too easy, as the client may become bored. Conversely, anything that is too difficult may become hard for a person to enjoy and can cause someone to give up out of frustration.

2. As mentioned earlier, avoid using punishments as they may keep a person from enjoying the workout routine.

3. Keep a person from being near too many people at a time.

Anyone who is surrounded by a large number of people may develop slight changes in workout routines or efforts. The principle of observational learning suggests that a person surrounded by too many others might be at risk of changing certain actions.

4. Review any irrational thoughts.

The irrational thoughts a person partakes in might cause someone to experience difficulties in a workout routine. These include problems where someone might fail to use the right principles for a workout or may become unrealistic about goals. Irrational thoughts should be replaced with newer thoughts that are more productive, thoughtful, positive and reasonable or realistic. Keeping those thoughts from being a threat will improve upon the likelihood of success.

5. While stimulus control may help, it is important to review how necessary or valuable the stimulus in question may be.

The stimulus should be examined carefully and then adapted as necessary.

6. A written agreement can be produced between you and the client.

The written agreement should be realistic and easy for a person to follow. When producing the agreement surrounding what can work in the routine, you have to incorporate that client into the mix. The client must have some kind of input as to what will go into the agreement, based on what that person is comfortable with handling and moving forward with.

7. Always review the SMART goal system.

Any goals that are to be produced in the process must be planned in accordance with the SMART standard. The rules involved will help people to stay comfortable and confident in the work they are putting in when trying to move forward.

Adding Support

Four forms of support may be provided to the participant during the workout process:

1. Instrumental

Instrumental support involves the basic and practical points that may be utilized to assist a person in achieving a goal.

2. Emotional

A person requires regular emotional support to continue to move forward. A sense of concern is needed regarding how well someone can keep a workout running.

3. Informational

Advice and directions on what should be done in the workout process should be discussed. Some information points may come from the CPT, but any other nutritional or health expert may be consulted. Print and online resources can also be incorporated in the workout, provided that the content involved is detailed and offers enough information for someone to use.

4. Companionship

People who are related to a participant in some way should be capable of getting into the same routine to support that person. The companionship involved can come from family members or from friends.

Self-Monitoring via Journal

Self-monitoring may be used in the workout routine to help a person with keeping tabs on a workout routine. The effort is designed to provide a person with the opportunity to handle the effort and to give that person a say in what will be done when working out. Self-monitoring identifies any progress that a person is putting in, or any lack of progress, if necessary. A person will have to engage in acts of self-reflection when looking at how a workout is going. Part of this includes being honest about the amount of work that one is putting in.

The practice requires a person to use a journal to keep track of the things that he or she is doing during a workout routine. The journal will keep a report of how well a workout plan is moving and will detail whether that person is dealing with any struggles or other concerns surrounding the workout. The journal should include the following points:

1. Write down details on when a workout took place. This includes the duration of that workout and how well it moved forward.
2. Discuss the efforts that were put into the workout. Write about the types of exercises that were put in, how many sets or reps were used, the rest periods in between each exercise and any feelings or sensations experienced during the process.
3. Talk about any particular things that took place during the workout. This includes any changes in environment or weather conditions relating to the event.
4. Discuss how the body felt, particularly whether any pains developed or dehydration was ever experienced.
5. A tally of one's weight or other physical features should be included. This can be updated regularly to see how well the workout routine is working.

The journaling process can work for as long as a person wants it to. The journal can be very detailed and elaborate if needed, although the data has to be focused based on a person's work. Any trends in the journal may be noticed by the participant. You may ask to review the journal, if need be, to figure out any trends that the participant has not noticed. This must only be done with that person's permission. Also, the process requires a participant to be honest and direct over the process. That person has to acknowledge any struggles that he or she is having, so it becomes easier for changes or adjustments to be made.

Ethical Concerns

The most important part of managing a relationship with a client is to ensure you are ethical and responsible. You must avoid forcing a person into a change unless that person has a significant medical concern that needs to be resolved as soon as possible. Be aware of how you talk with a person. Discuss specific ideas over what someone wishes to do when trying to stay healthy. Keep a participant's health considerations in mind and think about what someone prefers and has a desire to complete when figuring out a plan for managing fitness.

Questions

1. What should you notice when actively listening to a person?
    a. A person's rate of speech
    b. Any words a person places emphasis on
    c. Any suggestive points
    d. Verifiable points on a workout

2. Paraphrasing may be utilized when confirming what a person is saying. The key concept of paraphrasing involves:
    a. Repeating things exactly
    b. Reflecting on what someone says
    c. Questioning certain things
    d. Asking for confirmation

3. The main concept of the self-efficacy model involves a person's:
    a. Perception
    b. Desire for a healthy lifestyle
    c. Motivation
    d. Curiosity

4. A person in the transtheoretical model is currently thinking about a workout and what he or she can do. How long will it take, at most, for a person to actually move from that stage of contemplation to where he or she will start the workout?
    a. 1 month
    b. 3 months
    c. 6 months
    d. 1 year

5. A person who experiences a relapse at the maintenance stage of the transtheoretical model will move to this stage:
    a. Precontemplation
    b. Contemplation
    c. Preparation
    d. Action

6. A patient can be encouraged to do the following when monitoring his or her own improvements and efforts in the workout process:
    a. Prepare a journal
    b. Use a mobile app
    c. Workout with friends

    d. Have family members observe one's work

7. Outside of a CPT's effort, informational support may work best from the following groups
    a. Health journals
    b. Social media sites
    c. Self-help books
    d. All of the above

8. What can a written agreement for services include?
    a. Any terms for changing a workout format
    b. Ideas for what machines may work
    c. Any terms for breaking off the agreement
    d. Details on the workout routine that will be covered

9. The most common concern that may come out of irrational thoughts is that they are not only unrealistic but could also:
    a. Cause a person to enter into the wrong workout routine
    b. May keep a person from being willing to exercise
    c. Can make a person feel as though a certain workout routine will not be good enough
    d. All of the above

10. Shaping is different from observational learning in that, instead of learning by observing, shaping involves:
    a. Reviewing a person's thoughts
    b. Sticking to an agreement
    c. Progressive efforts in learning
    d. Noticing different actions among people

11. As a patient contemplates a workout, the person will have to look at:
    a. Nutritional concerns
    b. Emotional attitudes
    c. Effort points
    d. The type of routine one wishes to work with

12. Any changes that are to be made in the workout routine must only be enacted:
    a. Based on what the two parties agree to
    b. Based on what you say
    c. Under the whims of the participant
    d. When a doctor clears that person

13. When is it fine to punish someone during a workout or training routine?
    a. When that person does not meet his or her goals
    b. When that person does not complete exercises correctly
    c. When that person is not punctual in getting to a training session on time
    d. Never, if possible

14. The goal of negative reinforcement is to:
    a. Add to the challenge of a workout
    b. Remove any stimuli that may hurt one's progress
    c. Replace certain positive thoughts with more challenging thoughts
    d. Steer a person towards certain tasks

15. The difference between precontemplation and contemplation involves not only the timing involved but also:
    a. A person's general intentions
    b. Planning efforts
    c. Physical fitness
    d. Motivation

16. A vicarious experience that may develop in the fitness process involves a person being motivated by:
    a. News stories about health
    b. A CPT's work
    c. Another participant
    d. Personal beliefs

17. The self-efficacy model is often supported based on:
    a. Personal diet results
    b. How often a person works out
    c. Prior efforts working out
    d. What may be done in the future

18. In addition to helping people to relieve their stresses, Pilates may also be encouraged to help a person to:
    a. Focus on future workouts
    b. Tone muscles
    c. Improve flexibility
    d. Create a better relationship with a CPT trainer

19. Empathy produces positive emotions that:

a. Stop a person's body from fatigue
b. Correct any negative thoughts a person has
c. Show you understand the worries or concerns that a person has
d. Allow for a smart discussion over what a person is doing

20. The outcomes that may be produced when talking with a person should be:
    a. Realistic
    b. Related to the goals the person has
    c. Planned with a time frame the participant can follow
    d. All of the above

Answers

1. b. A person may place a strong emphasis on certain words due to feelings or attitudes over what is happening during a workout. Pay attention to whatever it is the person is placing emphasis on when figuring out problems.
2. b. Paraphrasing is not about repeating work but rather about reflecting on some statement or value that a person has put into the workout effort.
3. a. The self-efficacy model concentrates on what a person perceives to be valuable and useful when managing a workout the right way.
4. c. The six-month time frame is used, as this is a point where it may be easier for a person to plan ahead and to develop the interest and motivation needed to make significant long-term lifestyle changes.
5. d. A person could technically fall back into any of these points, but the most common type of relapse involves a person moving back by one stage to the one that was right before.
6. a. Although a mobile app may help keep tabs on information relating to the work that a person puts in, it is best for a person to use a journal for writing down information on what he or she is doing when working out. A journal may provide a person with more access to information on what he or she can do at a time.
7. d. Any source used for managing data can be employed, although it is best for a source to be thorough and comprehensive.
8. d. The key part of the agreement is to focus on the things relating to the workout that a person feels may be appropriate and useful for his or her fitness efforts.
9. d. Most of the irrational thoughts that people experience in their workout routines are unrealistic and nonsensical. They are followed solely because a person is afraid of what may happen in a workout routine.
10. c. The progression that comes with shaping may involve a person learning new ideas over an extended period without being fearful.

11. d. At this juncture in the planning process, a person will have a specific idea of what he or she wants to get out of a workout routine.
12. a. Teamwork is critical in the process of planning a physical fitness program. It is through this teamwork that it becomes easier for a program to be followed. Part of this includes ensuring that the two sides of a program are on the same page when getting a process moving forward with a general sense of understanding involved.
13. d. Punishments may be dangerous to the participant due to those punishments causing a person to feel worried or nervous over what he or she might be doing wrong in the workout process.
14. b. Instead of adding something that may harm a person, it is important to remove anything that causes negative feelings. Negative reinforcement involves finding and removing problems, not adding things that could make a problem worse or cause general concerns in a person.
15. a. The motivations that a person has will make a difference at this point. In the precontemplation stage, a person does not have any motivations. Those motivations will become prevalent in the contemplation process.
16. c. The work of a CPT will help anyone with growing a better sense of control over a workout, but it is through watching other people engage in fitness programs supported by a CPT that they will feel motivated to work hard and make the most out of their work.
17. c. Actual experiences and stimuli that a person has noticed should be observed, with an emphasis on any workouts a person has entered into, or other experiences that relate to what he or she is doing.
18. b. Pilates is useful for when a person wants to improve muscle tone while also finding a way to relax and rest. You can refer a person to a Pilates trainer if need be.
19. c. It is vital for you to notice how well you can identify a person's emotions and recognize how important they are to an individual. Empathy is about showing a person that you recognize the worries or issues that he or she has when trying to manage a healthy workout.
20. d. All outcomes should be reviewed based on what might be worthwhile and useful for a person's workout needs. This includes ensuring that the plans are sensible based on what you and your participant feel is right.

Domain 6: Professional Development and Responsibility

It is vital to recognize what you can do when looking to build your practice and make it work to your liking. There are several strategies that must be used to make it easier for your business to move forward. Many of these relate to the specific developmental plans that you wish to utilize.

Professional and Ethical Standards

Proper standards must be followed when aiming to develop your CPT business effort. You must ensure that all actions in the workplace are managed accordingly. All CPTs are required to follow the standards listed in the Code of Professional Conduct are listed by the National Academy of Sports Medicine. The code is designed to protect people from any negligent actions or other concerns that may develop during a training routine.

Professionalism

The Code of Professional Conduct requires the following standards for supporting a patient:

- All clients must be treated with the utmost respect possible.
- No assumptions should be made about any person based on behaviors, reasons for working out or how well a person can complete certain activities.
- The communication used between the CPT and the participant must be professional and carefully planned out.

Safety Standards

You must provide a safe environment for a person's workout. The following points are used in the Code of Professional Conduct for ensuring that a person's safety is safely managed:

- People who have certain health conditions should not undergo any training processes or efforts unless a person has been cleared to enter into certain physical activities.
- No diagnoses should be made regarding illnesses or injuries unless standard first aid is to be provided. A CPT can only make an official diagnosis if that person is legally licensed to be able to make such a declaration and if that person is working within a certain capacity for making a declaration at a time.

- In cases where someone experiences changes in medical history or feels sudden pain during regular training or workout sessions, that person should be referred to the appropriate medical practitioner. Any cases where sudden pain occurs or other concerns develop may require you to stop the training session.

- Proper hygiene is required. This includes seeing that a space is cleaned regularly.

- Any clothing that is to be worn should be modest and clean while ensuring the clothing is not going to get stuck on any equipment or otherwise inhibit the workout routine.

You must also use the proper emergency protocols to keep your business functional and responsible. Further details on these points will be listed later in this module for your convenience.

Confidentiality in Record Keeping

The code of conduct also states that the records that are gathered should be detailed, while at the same time being kept private. A CPT must handle the data carefully, based on:

- Physical issues
- Family histories relating to said issues
- Any preferences a person has for a workout routine
- Physical measurements that are relevant to the workout process

All data must be kept confidential and secure, without the information being given to other groups unless there is a medical review that has to take place from another entity. The data may also be provided to other parties in cases where it is legally required. Any minors who are being supported will have to provide voluntary consent via a third party. In most cases, this third party is the parent or guardian of the minor. The same process may also be considered for cases where a person is unable to give consent on his or her own. Any clients who are no longer being serviced should have their records securely stored. The content may also be privately destroyed depending on whether that person is to return or if there are any medical concerns that might need to be explored in the work process.

Legal and Ethical Points

The next part of the Code of Conduct focuses on the legal and ethical efforts that must be put into consideration during the work process:

- All local, state and federal considerations for operating a business should be followed. This is to ensure that people are legally protected from any ongoing concerns or legal issues that may develop.
- A business must be fully responsible for its actions. This includes responsibility for any conditions that may be dangerous or possibly likely to cause injuries or other kinds of harm.
- The records that are being tallied should be accurate and reflective of the people who use the services of a trainer. There should be no fabrications or edits involved with whatever is being offered at a time.
- Any property rights or intellectual data should be respected regarding the content and where it is from. A training service provider should be original, without trying to steal ideas or concepts from other competing groups.

The key part of handling a client's data is to ensure you get full permission from that person when doing anything for his or her needs. You must also recognize any threats to that person and find solutions that are made with that person's needs in mind, while also ensuring the safety of a person who wishes to move forward with a workout routine.

Business Practice Efforts

The Code of Conduct requires you to use several standards for managing a business and keeping it operational.

1. You must have liability insurance for keeping your business operational. This refers to insurance for covering any cases where you are held liable for damages or other injury-related concerns.
2. Proper progress notes should be provided to each client. These notes can be sent out as necessary and will be legitimate for most needs.
3. Any services that have been rendered should be discussed as evenly and accurately as possible.
4. All qualifications and affiliations that you hold must be discussed as truthfully and directly as possible.
5. You need to advertise your business in an honest manner while explaining all the terms and conditions relating to the services that you have to offer to people.
6. Proper financial and contractual data should be kept throughout the business. This includes keeping all financial receipts and data relating to clients for at least

four years, for the best results. You can keep that content in your office for a little longer if you feel someone has certain needs.

7. All rules relating to discrimination, harassment and other inappropriate activities must be followed. This includes avoiding any abusive or hostile actions that may create a potentially complicated or difficult environment that could be unfair to others.

Medical Clearance

Proper medical clearance is required for each person who wants to participate in a workout session. Clearance refers to confirming a person's ability to complete proper workouts without the risk of possible harm. A CPT must not clear a person for working out. Rather, a certified doctor or physician must confirm that a person can complete a workout routine. You will have to review the proper medical clearance forms that a person may provide you when planning a workout routine. The forms may include the most important details of:

1. Information on a patient's diagnosis
2. The name, address and contact information for the doctor that is clearing a person
3. Guidelines for a program

A physician will provide you with details on what parts of the body a person can work on, any limitations on range of motion and how much weight or stress the person can place on his or her body. The terms must be followed accordingly as you plan that person's workout routine. The person who provides the medical clearance may allow for certain changes to come about. You must not adjust the program unless the doctor or physician confirms that such changes are safe for a person.

4. Details on symptoms that a person might experience

Although a person should be confirmed for exercises, a doctor must also list information on the possible symptoms a person has with regards to any medical conditions. The symptoms must be listed clearly to give you an idea of what someone can handle at any given time.

5. Exceptions for efforts

Any specific exceptions that a person has should be listed. Such exceptions refer to particular exercises that have to be avoided. An explanation of why these points have to be avoided should be included in the clearance document.

6. Added comments

The doctor or physician can include as many additional comments or remarks regarding a person's physical efforts as necessary. These points may be incorporated to help explain what someone is entering into and what efforts may be produced when aiming to produce a better workout routine for someone to follow. You may contact the physician in question for extra details if needed.

Physical Appearance and Attire

You generally have the right to determine what should be utilized in a fitness training environment, but there are some standards that must be followed:

1. People should be prepared and ready for workouts with the proper attire. This includes basic fitness and active-wear outfits.

Clothes should cover enough of the body while also keeping the fabric from spreading out and creating a drag on a person's motions. Anything that is overly tight should be avoided. Tight clothing may inhibit a person's natural motions and could also cause a person to overheat depending on what happens in any situation.

2. The person's physical appearance should be reviewed based on cleanliness. A person should have properly washed off and been presentable

A person must be groomed accordingly, with hair tied up, if need be and with proper cleaning methods needed before the workout starts. A person will have to shower after the workout or fitness routine is finished. Showers may be provided at your training facility.

3. A person should ask for assistance with any issues relating to physical appearance.

Sometimes a person might have issues when his or her physical appearance has been negatively impacted due to issues relating to the body having gone through excess amounts of pressure from prior workouts. Be aware of any demands that someone might have for workout routines in the future to ensure certain problems that may come along can be resolved accordingly.

Punctuality

Proper reservations and times for sessions should be planned accordingly. All participants in your programs are expected to be on time or should at least arrive within a sensible time frame. You must also ensure that your business is open and ready for operation in any situation. The key is to provide a person with the proper time frame for a workout, without being complicated.

Business Development

Building a Client Base

You must be aware of how well you are working towards producing a stronger client base. The effort you put into getting your client base organized should be planned based on a series of segments.

General Marketing

Marketing can work in many forms. You can market a business through a basic online campaign or through local advertisements. Social media may also be planned. Further details on what to consider for your marketing efforts will be covered later in this domain.

Networking

Networking involves getting in touch with people and getting them to join your fitness program. You may talk with people who visit nutrition supply stores or gyms of all kinds. You can also talk with doctors in your area about who you can get to work with your fitness program. You have various controls over what you can do when marketing your work, but it is vital for you to notice what you are getting out of your work and how easy it may be to attract the clients that you want to your business. Your conversations when networking should focus on what you are offering to people, without trying to judge anyone's physical conditions. You can incorporate a person's medical history into the discussion if desired, but you should not touch upon that all too much or else you may add more stress or undue pressure to a person's mind at this juncture.

Financial Planning and Projects

You will have to review how your business will operate based on the funds you will use. The funds that are required for managing your work should help with covering points relating to the critical points for operating a business:

1. Review the equipment that you will use. This includes any workout machines that you will have people utilize.

2. Analyze the environment that your training programs will take place in. This includes the rent and maintenance costs involved.

3. You may consider having other people work for you as assistants if you wish. Review the costs associated with hiring people and paying them for their work. You may also look at the benefits they may be owed.

4. Liability insurance costs and other legal expenses should also be reviewed as you plan your budget.

You can produce projections over what your business is doing through forecasting. This process involves using certain percentages for work based on the prior financial performances you have noticed in your workplace.

Planning for Income

You may use an analytical process for figuring out what you can do when aiming to get more money and to reach your financial goals.

1. Figure out the annual income you are aiming for.
2. Review the earnings you must bring in each week in order to attain that income goal.
3. Figure out the number of sessions needed to get there. You can review the funds you charge for each session to get an estimate at this point.
4. Factor in the expenses relating to keeping your organization running accordingly.

After you plan your analysis, you can work toward finding people who may be interested in the services you are offering.

5. Figure out how many people you need to get into your office each week. This includes both the new people who will work with you and any existing clients that you regularly meet with.
6. Break down the interactions you will have with all of these people by the hour.
7. Ask for contact information for each person you interact with. You may use this contact information later on if there is a potential for you to have a special deal or term set up with someone who may be interested in your workout services.

Four Ideas to Use When Planning Your Marketing Efforts

Review how well your business marketing plans are organized so you can help people to recognize what makes your business useful to them. This section focuses on four ideas that you may utilize when you plan on your marketing efforts and getting people to notice what you are offering.

1. **Product**

Start by focusing on the type of product you wish to offer. This may include:

- Access to workout machines
- New equipment for workout needs
- A variety of weights for lifting
- A convenient and safe environment for workouts
- Your expertise in planning workout routines

Your promotional efforts should be based on what makes your work unique while letting people see what makes your business is so valuable and worth contacting for assistance.

2. Price

The price that will be charged should be analyzed accordingly. The price should be organized based on:

- The unique nature of what you are offering
- How advanced your services are
- What it costs for you to get your equipment ready
- A general comparison of what your competitors might be charging for services

Keep the price as fair as possible so people will be more interested in what you are offering. You should avoid using any unrealistic prices, but it is also important to see that the prices are reflective of what you have to offer and that they are sensible for the demands that people have. The most important thing is to let people know that your services have a value attached to them and that what you are offering should be interesting and useful to the people that you wish to help. Be prepared to market your price well when trying to make your work more visible and helpful for people.

3. Place

The place that your CPT services are offered should be analyzed accordingly. You may consider various places for getting your work ready:

- A gym that you may establish an agreement to operate out of
- A private office that you have access to; this can include a dedicated fitness training spot that is separate from what you may find in a gym
- Any spots in your home; this may work if you have a private gym or other workout space available in your home

- Any open spaces for a workout, including park spaces; these may be considered last, as these are public spots that are not as properly controlled as what you might find from other locations for workout use

Your marketing efforts can include a promotion of the business location and what makes the place special for training needs. Explaining to the client what makes the location useful and what features come with that can help influence a positive decision. You may also talk about the convenience of the location, if possible. This is particularly for cases where you are located in an area near major roads and business centers or communal areas of note.

4. Promotion

The promotional aspect refers to the types of messages or special offers you plan on giving out to people who may be interested in your work. You can use a promotional effort to highlight your business to other people by focusing on what makes your business special and inviting for use. You may promote your business by focusing on a very specific or unique selling point that makes your business more inviting to the average client. You can talk about points such as these:

- How long you have been working as a CPT
- What types of concepts you want to help people with as you train them
- The types of equipment you have to offer and what makes them so helpful
- How your business compares with other entities; avoid referring to very specific competitors in this case
- The pricing points you wish to offer to clients who wish to use your services

Be direct when talking with others about what you wish to offer. You have to show that whatever you are highlighting is interesting for people to find and that you have interesting services that are worth promoting. Using these four pillars of marketing should assist you in planning a better effort in marketing and showing people what makes your work special.

Sales Concepts and Techniques

You must review what you can do when aiming to get people to notice your work. This segment of the domain focuses on how you are going to reach people who may be interested in what you are offering and explaining to them why your work will be so useful to them.

Lead Generation

Your first goal for sales is to look at the leads that you are looking to produce. You have to produce leads to find people who may be interested in the workout and fitness routine services you wish to promote. These main points must be used when finding leads:

1. Visit places that people who are interested in improving upon their bodies may visit.

You can visit a local health goods or physical care store to find people who may be interested in your services. Such a store may include products for sale that focus mainly on how a person's body can be improved upon through basic workouts.

2. Talk with people about the physical needs that they might have.

You can discuss how well people are managing their routines and what they are doing to succeed. The important part of this process is that you have an idea of what you wish to offer to others and that you understand the requirements that people have for their health demands.

3. Follow up with people after you make an initial contact. The discussion may include reaching people who are interested in your work and are available to meet with you again.

Having a follow-up conversation with a lead that you have gotten in the past is vital for helping people to see that you are legitimately interested in their health and that you want to offer services that you feel are appropriate for their needs.

Presenting

The presenting process should focus on explaining your business to people and what makes it special. You must be visible when promoting your work and showing what makes it different from other services. As you present your work, you must be willing to not only talk about your business in detail but also be persistent in asking for a sale. It is easier to lose a sale if you do not ask for it while in the presenting stage. Offer a sale to let the client know that you are committed to his or her health and that you are actively trying to make something available to others who might develop a vested interest in whatever is being offered.

Overcoming Objections

There is a potential that possible customers might object to certain things in your business. A few essential points may be used to overcome any objections that people might have to what you are offering:

1. Talk with the client about the concerns.

A person might object to what you are offering because that person is not comfortable with whatever is being offered. You can talk with that person about the issues surrounding whatever is being offered. Be open about the problems and ask about whatever he or she thinks can be done to resolve the issue at hand.

2. Figure out the real problem that a person has.

Sometimes problems might be superficial, but in other cases, some problems may be real. These include problems like a fear of not having a good workout, uncertainty over how well your service may work or even issues and worries about the price for services. Focusing on the real problem is critical for understanding the needs that someone has.

3. Remind the client about why that person needs to make changes.

The changes that a client needs to be made for the sake of good health should be discussed. A person might have certain physical issues that need to be corrected. Perhaps that someone has an increased likeliness of developing a medical condition. The concerns that a person has must be addressed to acknowledge what can be done to resolve anything that a person wants to manage in a workout process.

4. Resolve the situation by producing a sensible plan.

You can create any kind of plan you want to work with. You can talk with a client about workout routines that can be prepared and what can be done for maintaining his or her health in any form. An appropriate plan may be reviewed to figure out what should be done

Equipment Maintenance and Safety

All equipment that will be utilized in your workout environment must be maintained and kept safe and easy for all to use. Failure to keep the equipment protected and safe for all could result in you being liable for damages or possible negligence. You may use a checklist for planning a safer workout space for people to participate in:

1. Keep all flooring surfaces safe and clear. The floors should be clean, smooth and strong enough to handle anyone's foot movements without risking any slippage.
2. Analyze the equipment in your workplace. All wires and cables on machines must be sturdy and not at risk of breaking apart. All weights should also be full and not include any cracks or other imperfections that may cause injury or an imbalance in a workout.
3. Review the lighting in your environment. The lighting should be bright enough to where everyone in a space can see where they are going while not being at risk of falling over any surfaces.

4. Allow for ventilation in the environment. Air must move through fans or air-conditioning vents, among other items. The ventilation is required for keeping people from overheating while working out.

Time Frames for Billing

You can bill people based on the services they use and how often they get in touch with you. This schedule for billing should be focused based on the services that people actually utilize. Do not try to charge people if they are injured or hospitalized for any reason while on a program you have designed. This would be a highly unprofessional action if handled improperly.

Emergency Situation Protocols

All persons should be vetted before starting a routine, to identify any risks involved so proper decisions can be made to reduce the risk of any substantial threats that may come about while trying to complete a successful workout.

Assessing the Emergency

The emergency in question must be examined in detail to identify any possible problems.

1. The ABC Check

There are three parts of the ABC check:

- **Airway** – Review how well the patient's airways are working. This includes seeing that air is moving out of the respiratory system.
- **Breathing** – The breathing should be nominal, although any irregularities should be identified.
- **Circulation** – The patient's circulation may be inhibited due to an injury. The lack of circulation may cause damage to an area that is at risk of harm.

The exam can be used quickly, although the issues around a person's body during an emergency should be easy to notice.

2. Full body analysis

A person's body should be examined for swelling, tenderness or any deformities that have developed. You may need to take a person's pulse.

3. Blood pressure test

Sometimes a blood pressure test may be required in some cases. The test should help you with identifying if someone is experiencing hypertension or hypotension. You will need to contact the appropriate emergency authorities in your area if a person has experienced a dramatic injury and needs immediate medical attention.

AED Usage

An automated external defibrillator is vital for use in your clinic. An AED is an electronic device that identifies arrhythmias and other sudden heart-related concerns. The AED will correct cases of ventricular fibrillation, a heart rhythm dysfunction that develops when the heart is unable to manage regular physical functions. The VF issue should be converted back into a regular heart rhythm after the AED is used. This must work within the first three to five minutes of VF for the best results. The heart's functionality should restart after the AED is used. You must still contact emergency authorities after using the AED. This is to allow the patient to be fully monitored further and to identify any other possible physical issues that might have developed due to the issue that developed.

Handling Specific Concerns

There are many rules for taking care of very specific medical emergencies:

Respiratory Distress

A person experiencing respiratory issues will develop issues where the chest is not expanding or contracting during the natural breathing process. A person's nostrils may start to flare up as that person attempts to try and breathe. The neck muscles may start to strain from the added pressure. Cyanosis, a condition that entails a bluish tone around the lips and nose, among other parts of the body, may also develop. The skin can look pale or feel sweaty. At this point, a patient might require CPR to attempt to move air back into the respiratory system. You must also contact emergency authorities if there are significant problems with the person's airways. The patient may recover after resting, but you should contact medical professionals for help if the patient is struggling to recover.

Choking

A person's airway may become blocked while exercising. This could be a sign of choking as that person becomes hypoxic or unable to take in enough oxygen. In this case, the Heimlich maneuver may be performed on the patient. This should help with removing the item that is blocking the airway and allow air to move through once more.

Asthma

Asthma is a problem where a person experiences chronic inflammation in the airway. The inflammation will cause a person to develop shortness of breath and coughing. A person should be allowed to rest if he or she experiences a sudden asthma attack during a workout routine. A person with asthma should go through lighter exercises to keep the airways from being at risk of harm. The workout area should also be clean and comfortable, with no allergens.

Heart Attack

A person who undergoes an immense amount of physical activity may be at risk of developing a heart attack. In this case, a person will develop shortness of breath while experiencing pains around the neck, left arm, shoulder and stomach areas. Chest pains develop among people who have heart attacks; these pains are especially pronounced among women. A person who is having a heart attack must be immediately sent to a hospital for treatment.

Fainting

A person will faint when that person develops a lack of blood flow into the brain. This may come about due to dehydration, intense stress or pain or high body temperature. A person may be sent to an area to rest and to cool off. Proper cold compresses may be added to the body if needed, although hydration is best. The issues should not require a person to be sent to a hospital, although this may be required in cases where a person does not recover from the fainting spell within a reasonable amount of time. The patient may also request that you contact a proper medical authority. You must follow through on the request immediately.

Stroke

A stroke can develop in cases where a blood vessel in the brain becomes blocked. The condition may develop due to blood vessels not forming accordingly. An aneurysm may also develop as a growth or bubble within the vessel will rupture and break apart. A person who experiences a stroke will experience the following concerns:

- Weakness in one part of the body
- Numbness around some extremities; this may be noticed in the face
- Slurred speech or difficulties with talking
- Issues with walking
- The person's balance not being correct
- Intense headache
- Vision loss

Emergency services must be contacted as soon as possible to control the issue. The condition has to be resolved as soon as possible as the permanent damage resulting from the stroke may be worse if treatment is not administered soon.

Heat Stroke or Stress

A person who becomes too warm may develop heat stroke or stress. The condition may be aggravated by intense workouts or high temperatures. A person may develop a weak pulse or hypotension. A person can also become weak and develop an intense headache. The person's body temperature may be 104 degrees Fahrenheit or 40 Celsius at this point. The following must be done when a person experiences heat stroke or stress:

- Stop the exercise routine immediately.
- Remove the patient's clothing and cool him or her immediately.
- Give cold fluids, particularly water.
- Elevate the feet by about 12 to 18 inches.
- Monitor the patient's temperature. In cases where the temperature gets to over 105 degrees, the person should be sent to a hospital for further treatment.

Hyperglycemia

Patients with diabetes may be at risk of developing hyperglycemia or high blood sugar. A person will become exceptionally thirsty and fatigued at this point. A person should be provided with water at this point. The person should also stop working out immediately.

Hypoglycemia

Hypoglycemia is a condition where a person has a low blood sugar level. A person may become weak or fatigued and may experience intense hunger. A headache may also be present. About 20 to 30 carbs of carbohydrates should be provided to a person at the first sign of the condition. The carbohydrates must be low in fat for the best results. The patient's blood glucose level should be measured regularly before that person can go back to exercising. The level should be 100 mg/dL or greater before returning to work.

Soft-Tissue Injuries

A person who experiences a soft-tissue injury may experience significant pain and be at risk of infection, depending on the issue. Soft-tissue injuries that may develop in the workout include the following, arranged in order of increasingly severity:

- **Abrasion.** The injury is a basic scrape that can develop following a fall.
- **Incision.** A sharp edge or other pointed surface may cut into the tissue.
- **Laceration.** A tensile force causes a tear to develop in the soft tissue.
- **Avulsion.** This is an intense laceration where the skin is torn apart from the rest of the tissue.
- **Puncture.** The skin is penetrated by a sharp object.

Proper first aid should be provided at the start; this includes cleaning the impacted area with rubbing alcohol and then using a proper covering to secure the area that experienced the injury. A person may be sent to a hospital in the event that the injury is significant and might have impacted any organs or deep tendons. The person should also rest while trying to recover from the injury, to keep the injury from worsening.

Fracture

A fracture of a bone develops when intense pressure is added to the structure. This may also occur when a person falls. Fractures can develop from a person handling more weight than he or she should be, or possibly from losing his or her balance during a workout. People who are older, or those who have osteoporosis, are at an elevated risk.

A fracture may be noticed by:

- Any deformed features around the body; in the most significant cases, a bone end may be noticeable
- A joint not working properly; the joint may be stuck in one position
- Crepitus, a condition where bone fragments grind upon each other after a break
- Swelling and bruising around the injured site

When a person experiences a fracture, you must keep the area elevated and ensure the person does not move the area. Contact emergency professionals.

Professional Limitations of Personal Training

You may be limited as to what you can do when taking care of a patient. You must provide a person with proper access to other authorities when it comes to managing his or her body. As a CPT, you are certified to produce a fitness and training program for a person. You must refer a person to another professional if that person ever needs additional help, such as:

- **Psychologist.** You can refer a person to a psychologist for further counseling if need be. This is for cases when the person's health-related issues might become exacerbated due to stress or other ongoing issues.

- **Dietician.** While you can talk with a person about the meals and how certain dietary plans may be organized, it is best for that person to talk with a dietician. The dietician can recommend certain dietary routines.

- **Physician.** Only a certified doctor may diagnose any injuries a person has. You may use initial care for helping to keep a person comfortable, depending on the suspected injury, but you are not capable of legally determining if that a person has a very specific injury. A physician will review the concern and can then determine any proper long-term treatment required for controlling the issue.

Requirements for Maintaining Your Credentials

You will have to maintain a few standards in order to remain credentialed as a CPT:

- Renew your CPR and AED certification every two years.

- Obtain two or more continuing education credits relating to your field.

- Complete a recertification application to continue to maintain your credentials. Again, this must take place every two years.

For additional resources on CPT rules and regulations, you can check with the National Academy of Sports Medicine to learn what you need to about managing services for patients who require help with maintaining their bodies.

Resources of Information for Health and Fitness Education

You may use the following resources for added information:

1. Journals

You can review journals such as *Physical Therapy* and the *Journal of Orthopedic and Sports Physical Therapy* for additional details on the CPT field. The journals include many peer- reviewed and scholarly reports relating to the industry.

2. Continuing education courses

You will have to continue to complete regular continuing education courses to remain certified in your field. Such courses should provide you with new information on the

CPT field. You can find information on such courses online; these include courses that are certified by NASM or the National Strength and Conditioning Association (NSCA).

3. Conferences and workshops

Conferences and workshops are held by the NASM and NSCA, among many other CPT-related organizations. The events will provide you with networking opportunities and information on the latest trends relating to regular workout efforts.

Opportunities for Professional Growth

You have many considerations to review when it comes to your possible professional growth:

1. **Resumé writing**

You may consider reviewing your résumé to see how well your experiences with managing the physical needs of patients may work. You can plan a quality résumé that lets people identify what you are doing in the field and what services you have to offer.

2. **Opportunities in fitness centers**

You may consider working with different fitness centers or gyms as a CPT if desired. This may work well if you do not have the ability to be an independent contractor just yet.

3. **Personal equipment investments**

You can purchase your own pieces of workout equipment to use. This may work in cases where you are trying to help people with managing their workouts without having to resort to using other people's equipment. You may consider operating your own business after a while, although this will require an added investment and more experience to create a positive environment that is supportive for the workout routines and needs that each person might have over time.

Test Questions and Answers

1. What should be done about any assumptions that you may come across when helping a person?
    a. Get rid of them
    b. Ask questions
    c. Figure out how rational they are
    d. Talk with other specialists

2. Can you make a diagnosis of any illnesses or injuries?
    a. Yes
    b. In most cases
    c. Only if you are certified or licensed
    d. Never

3. How long should you keep records when it comes to handling the information your clients provide you with?
    a. 2 years
    b. 4 years
    c. 6 years
    d. For as long as necessary

4. A doctor's exemption note should include details on what a participant is capable of doing. What should you do if the doctor does not list a certain thing of interest?
    a. Contact the doctor for further information
    b. Talk with the person about the issue
    c. Avoid participating in that action
    d. Proceed with caution

5. What is the best type of activewear for a person to have when getting ready to work with you?
    a. Basic casual clothing
    b. Tight apparel
    c. Fitted clothes that don't hang too much
    d. Certain parts of apparel can be skipped if preferred

6. What type of networking activity works best when trying to target people at a nutrition supplement store?
    a. Offer flyers to people who come into the store
    b. Talk with people about what you are offering
    c. Recommend certain products

    d. Discuss medical conditions

7. When promoting your product, you may talk about the workout equipment you have for people to use. You must place an emphasis on:
    a. General access
    b. Technical features
    c. Types of machines
    d. Weight totals

8. What can you do when figuring out a price you wish to promote for your services?
    a. Compare it with other competitors
    b. List the rationale for the price
    c. Explain any payment plans you offer
    d. Discuss the payment options you accept

9. What is the best possible place for you to have your practice?
    a. At a training facility
    b. In your home
    c. At a park
    d. A and B

10. You can talk about the workout equipment you have to offer if you wish, but you must do this with the following point in mind:
    a. A focus on the variety of workouts your equipment can support
    b. How modern or unique your work is
    c. Why your equipment is critical for the success of a person's workout
    d. How much weight can be supported by your equipment

11. You can talk with people about their physical demands while generating leads. The process must be utilized as a means of:
    a. Planning a new marketing ploy
    b. Showing empathy or interest in a person's needs
    c. Creating new plans for working out on the spot
    d. Figuring out if a person is at risk of harm

12. When you come across an objection, you will have to let a person know what the problems are with a workout. Part of this includes:
    a. Understanding why a person is worried about a program
    b. Recognizing a person's medical needs
    c. Looking at the person's budget
    d. Figuring out how enthusiastic a person is about a program

13. You have revived a person in the workout environment with an AED device. What should you do next?
    a. Call medical authorities
    b. Elevate the person's head
    c. Allow the person to cool off
    d. Turn the person on his or her side

14. A person who is on a program that you have planned is in the hospital for a medical condition. What should you do about the funds that the person owes you for prior services?
    a. Continue to charge the person
    b. Waive the charges
    c. Wait until the person has properly recovered
    d. Talk with the person's doctor

15. When should you bring a person who has fainted in your care to the hospital?
    a. Right away
    b. If that person does not recover within a short period
    c. No need to do so
    d. When the person asks for it

16. A person may develop droopiness around one's face during a stroke. The droopiness is noted for being:
    a. Immediate
    b. On one part of the face
    c. Accentuated by a light tone
    d. Accentuated by sweating

17. A person may be diagnosed as having heat stress if that person's temperature reaches this point in Fahrenheit:
    a. 101
    b. 102
    c. 103
    d. 104

18. What should be done to help a person who experiences a hypoglycemic attack during a workout?
    a. Immediately provide a small amount of carbs
    b. Allow that person to walk off the issue
    c. Place a cold compress on the person's body

d. See how long it takes for that person to get back to regular lifting or workout activity

19. The following soft-tissue injury is the most significant and may require immediate help from a hospital:
    a. Puncture
    b. Incision
    c. Abrasion
    d. Avulsion

20. A person who experiences a fracture should be taken to a hospital as soon as possible. What should you do with the patient while waiting for the proper medical authorities to arrive?
    a. Keep the patient on his or her side
    b. Allow that person to stay in the same spot
    c. Try to move the bone structure as close to its original place as possible
    d. Elevate the injured body part

Answers

1. a. The Code of Professional Conduct states that you must not try to make any assumptions about what someone might be doing or what can be handled when trying to help a person.
2. c. You can only work with a diagnosis if you have been certified to work with other medical procedures or functions. In other cases, you should only perform first aid when taking care of a person's needs following an injury or other significant concern.
3. b. You can get rid of any old reports for at least four years. You have the option to get rid of those reports and data points after the four-year mark, but you can also keep that data on hand for as long as desired.
4. c. The best thing to do is to avoid trying to force certain actions on a patient until it is deemed safe to allow that person to engage in a certain physical activity.
5. c. It is best to ensure that a person can physically handle the exercises involved without wearing anything that might be restrictive and could cause a person to overheat. Comfortable clothes should be planned accordingly.
6. b. The focus when networking is to highlight what you have to offer and how your services may be to the benefit of whoever may require that assistance.
7. a. Place emphasis on general access to the things you are interested in highlighting.
8. a. Allow for a discussion of what your competitors are offering, but do not mention specific names. You can say that your services are discounted when compared with what others have to offer, for instance.

9. d. Although a park has enough room for many activities, it is often best for you to use a private space that might be a little easier to control.
10. c. Do not be specific when talking about the certain workout machines you have to offer. You only need to talk about the specific movements that someone can use when handling a workout machine in the right way.
11. b. You have to immediately state any relationship you have with another entity. This includes showing that you recognize the needs that people hold and that what is being offered will be more valuable for them.
12. a. A participant might be worried about what is being offered. This includes worries over how a program might not be as useful or efficient as he or she might wish. You can talk about the concerns someone has and then find ways about how they can be resolved through your program, but this must also be done in a non-confrontational or non-judgmental manner.
13. a. Even if any sudden heart irregularities are resolved, you have to contact medical authorities to have them bring the person to a hospital. The event that caused you to use the AED may be a sign of a significant medical concern.
14. c. You have the option to waive a person's debts to you, but the best thing to do is to wait until that person has recovered. At that point, you can determine if that person can continue to work with you and whether it is fair or not for you to continue to be paid for whatever services you offered. Whatever the case, avoid forcing a payment in this situation.
15. b. You should wait for a person to recover properly, although you can also listen to that person's needs for being sent out to a doctor if needed.
16. b. The drooping may be more noticeable in one part of the face than any other. The issue may spread to other parts of the face, depending on what happens.
17. d. Any person who experiences a sudden rise to 105 degrees should be sent to a doctor immediately. Those who are still at the 104 mark need to be provided with rest and cold fluids, specifically water.
18. a. About 20 to 30 grams of carbs should be provided to the patient at this point. This may help improve the blood glucose level in the immediate moment.
19. a. The puncture moves deeper into the body than other injuries that one might experience. The condition may entail damages to an organ, depending on how intense the situation is. An abrasion only occurs on the outermost part of the body and may be treated on site in a few moments with rubbing alcohol and a proper dressing.
20. d. Allowing the spot to remain elevated ensures that the pressure felt in the region will not be as intense. The process may improve upon how well the patient is treated.

Pretrial Questions

1. The global stabilization system is a part of the body that does the following for managing stresses:
    a. Moves loads from the upper to middle parts of the body
    b. Supports general balance functions in most workouts
    c. Keeps people from experiencing intense fatigue in a workout
    d. Enhances how the body takes in fluids for hydration

2. The local stabilization system includes all but the following muscles:
    a. Diaphragm
    b. Pelvis floor
    c. Internal oblique
    d. Gluteus medius

3. The epiphysis, inside the skeletal system, is utilized to help with:
    a. Linking bones together
    b. Allowing bones to be replaced
    c. Shaping joints
    d. Supporting a basic range of motion

4. Although testosterone may help with improving how well the body can produce added muscle mass, this may also cause problems relating to:
    a. Added hair growth
    b. Deepening of the voice
    c. Firmness around the body
    d. All of the above

5. The following gate among voltage-gated cells in the nervous system focuses on activating cells:
    a. M
    b. H
    c. N
    d. T

6. The pleural cavity in the body will develop changes in pressure based on:
    a. Stress in a workout
    b. Body temperature
    c. Compression
    d. Inhalation and exhalation

7. Anaerobic exercises are to be completed during this amount of time in an average set:

a. 15 seconds
b. 30 seconds
c. 1 minute
d. 2 minutes

8. What is the best place to consider when finding new information relating to your field of work?
    a. Academic journals
    b. Social media sites
    c. Networking with others
    d. Talking with patients

9. What should you renew every two years, alongside your CPT certification?
    a. Citizenship papers
    b. Medical insurance policy
    c. CPR and AED certification
    d. Liability insurance policy

10. What can you do when talking with someone about the dietary needs that he or she has?
    a. Recommend certain supplements
    b. Prescribe medications
    c. Refer a person to a dietician
    d. Write a diet plan

11. Crepitus occurs when the bones:
    a. Grind against each other due to an injury
    b. Grind against each other due to arthritis
    c. Protrude out of their sockets
    d. Trigger swelling

12. An avulsion is a type of tear in the body where the skin:
    a. Tears from the rest of the body
    b. Is impacted
    c. Develops intense bleeding that does not clot easily
    d. Becomes entangled with an indentation in the bone structure

13. People who have diabetes should not undergo SMR procedures due to:
    a. Vein damages to the legs
    b. Nerve issues
    c. Possibly blood complications
    d. Added fatigue

14. When is the right time to allow some sense of progression in a workout routine?
    a. When the person has mastered a certain exercise
    b. When that person has reached a plateau in a certain process
    c. If the person is feeling bored with exercises that he or she has utilized for a while
    d. All of the above

15. A single-effort lift can entail this many reps in a power exercise:
    a. 2
    b. 3
    c. 4
    d. 5

16. A body will lose its strength at this rate when compared with the rate that it gains strength:
    a. Half as quickly
    b. About the same rate
    c. Twice as fast
    d. Three times as fast

17. A person should move forward with a more intense workout routine if the heart rate is:
    a. Elevated
    b. Consistent
    c. Too low
    d. Sporadic

18. A PAR-Q assessment should review whether a person is taking medications for:
    a. Diabetes
    b. Lung functions
    c. Sexual performance
    d. Blood pressure

19. The back may be observed in a person who has been sitting down while working for far too long. A person who has a posture issue may develop this feature in the back:
    a. Rounding
    b. Uneven shoulders
    c. Inflammation
    d. Stiffness

20. A person's bowel movements may be discussed, if necessary. You can refer a person to a doctor if that someone is experiencing:
    a. Increased urination
    b. Changes in how many times he or she uses the bathroom
    c. Any issues relating to constipation
    d. Any problems he or she might have in general

Answers

1. a. Muscles such as the psoas major, external obliques and quadratus lumborum are included in this section of the body.
2. d. The gluteus medius is a part of the global stabilization system. The other parts are all featured in the local stabilization system.
3. a. Ossification is required for getting bones to connect with each other within the process of keeping the bones sturdy.
4. d. Testosterone is a male hormone and therefore can cause some male characteristics to become present in a person's body. This is unless the hormone is organized accordingly.
5. a. The M gate is responsible for opening voltage connections between cells in the nervous system. As the nervous system is triggered, the gate will allow many signals to move along. The H gate stops voltages while the N gate focuses on depolarized cells.
6. d. The pleural cavity will develop less pressure as a person inhales. The pressure level will rise when the person exhales.
7. a. Anaerobic exercises are designed to work in as little time as possible to secure the body's natural functionality for movement.
8. a. You may have an easier time learning about newer and more technical points relating to taking care of patients through advanced academic journals relating to your field.
9. c. Regular certification of your AED and CPR skills is needed to confirm that you recall how these processes work and what you must do when carrying them out.
10. c. Although you can talk about some of the nutritional things that one needs for a workout and provide ideas, you must refer a person to a dietician in this case. A dietician can talk with someone about what may be done when resolving certain issues relating to a person's body.
11. a. The grinding sounds can be immediately noticed in many cases where a person is trying to recover from an injury. The sound is a sign that a person has broken something and that proper treatment is needed.

12. a. The injury is similar to what you may experience in a laceration, except the impact involved will be more significant and disruptive to the body's natural functions.
13. b. Issues with nerves around the body may cause significant concerns in some patients. The problems may be more pronounced among those who have foot-related issues or who have been at a risk of amputation in that part of the body.
14. d. The key part of progression is that it allows people to move forward with their work and prevents any possible worries or issues a person might have.
15. a. A lower number of reps may be used in this case when compared with a multiple-effort lift that requires more reps.
16. a. It takes longer for muscle gains to be reversed, but those who continue to work with regular lifting routines will be at less of a risk of significant issues when trying to manage a workout the right way.
17. c. A person's heart rate has to be elevated during the workout process to improve upon his or her success in a workout. Proper changes may be made to the workout routine if a person is not doing well with the heart rate.
18. d. Although a person should talk with you about all the medications that he or she is taking, you should place extra caution on how the individual's blood pressure is being managed and whether any medications are being used for controlling the issue.
19. a. Rounding may occur from the shoulders moving forward far too much when the tissues are activated.
20. All bowel-related problems must be discussed, no matter what. You can have a person talk with a doctor about the concern if needed. Referring a person to a doctor is appropriate as you are not supposed to diagnose a person's medical issues.

Assessment Questions

1. Pattern overload develops when a person:
    a. Lifts the same amount of weight all the time
    b. Works for the same period of time in a session
    c. Keeps making the same repeated motions
    d. Sits in a spot for too long

2. A person who experiences visceral pain is experiencing pains in:
    a. Nerves
    b. Organs
    c. Soft tissues
    d. Around the skin

3. A sleep exam, in an elements of lifestyle questionnaire, may include an analysis of all of the following points:
    a. Wake and sleep cycles
    b. How rested a person is after waking up
    c. When that person gets to sleep
    d. The amount of time needed to get to sleep

4. A Rockport walk test is best for use among:
    a. Obese patients
    b. Younger participants
    c. Seniors
    d. People with diabetes

5. The MHR for a person should be greater among:
    a. Younger patients
    b. Seniors
    c. Pregnant women
    d. People with diabetes

6. Pronation may be identified in a patient during an analysis of how the knees and feet are functioning during a workout or through natural physical movements. Pronation may be identified by:
    a. How far forward or backward the tissues move out
    b. How well a person's muscles bend
    c. The speed of the movement
    d. Slight rotations of the tissues during a walk

7. A circumference test may be utilized if a person has:
    a. Varicose veins
    b. Inflammation
    c. Sweating
    d. A sizeable gut

8. A person's power level may need to be tested to identify how well that person can handle certain workouts and to assess whether that person is capable of moving to the power stage of a workout routine. The following test may be used to analyze this:
    a. 1-repetition maximum
    b. Shark skill test
    c. Davies test
    d. Vertical jump

9. The shark skill test results may be measured based on:
    a. How long a person goes through the exercise
    b. How a person stays within the boxes
    c. The order of boxes handled
    d. Any cases where a person struggles with balance

10. The cones in the LEFT test should be placed this far apart from each other:
    a. 10 yards
    b. 20 yards
    c. 30 yards
    d. 40 yards

11. An overheat squat should be analyzed based on a person's ability to handle all but the following:
    a. Keeping the knees and feet straight
    b. Keeping the lower back steady
    c. How the shoulders are positioned
    d. The weight's ability to stay on a certain base

12. A person completing a single-leg squat should experience the following with the hip:
    a. No adduction
    b. A slight pronation
    c. Protrusions
    d. Changes in elevation

13. For the best results, the following may be done during a gait test:
    a. Video recording of the movements
    b. Changes in the slope
    c. Speed adjustments on occasion
    d. Electrode use

14. A person who is undergoing a gait test may be analyzed further if the following develops:
    a. Steady head position
    b. The knees and feet are not pronating
    c. The LPHC rotates
    d. The shoulders are straight and not rounded

15. A lateral view is used in the pulling test to identify how the body is positioned. The lower back can be reviewed in this case to identify the following issue:
    a. The back staying straight
    b. The back arching
    c. Changes in muscle texture while lifting
    d. Irritation or inflammation

16. The fat mass is measured by taking a person's body-fat percentage and multiplying it by:
    a. Weight
    b. Height
    c. Age
    d. Gender variable

17. A BMI test may identify if a person is overweight or obese, but it may be misleading based on a person's:
    a. Age
    b. Gender
    c. Lean muscle mass
    d. Bone density

18. What should you do about managing a participant's diet?
    a. Produce caloric restrictions
    b. Prescribe supplements
    c. Have a person use a food diary
    d. Refer a person to a dietician

19. A CPT can diagnose a person as having a certain medical condition if the CPT:
    a. Identifies sudden changes in the body
    b. Notices differences in a workout
    c. Identifies pain
    d. Is certified for diagnosing that person

20. A patient's workout routine can be adjusted:
    a. When that person is doing better with workouts
    b. When someone has a new goal
    c. Every four weeks
    d. All of the above

21. The skinfold measurements for identifying subcutaneous fat deposits should be performed:

a. On the right side of the body
b. Along the extremities
c. At the waist area
d. Through electroanalysis

22. A patient is complaining of shoulder pains. An anterior or posterior view of the shoulders can be conducted to identify the following issue in a person's posture:
    a. How level the shoulders are
    b. Any protrusions around the shoulders
    c. How well the neck is laid out
    d. Changes in the spinal column

23. A positive resting heart rate should be at the following beats per minute:
    a. 65
    b. 75
    c. 85
    d. 95

24. A woman who begins a program with you regularly wears dress shoes. Her feet should be reviewed based on:
    a. Heel fatigue
    b. Pronation
    c. Swelling
    d. Nerve damage

25. A man beginning a workout routine reports that he spends much of his work day sitting down at a desk. His body can be reviewed for all but the following:
    a. Head position
    b. How rounded the shoulders are
    c. The tightness around the hip flexors
    d. Whether the knees are protruding or pronating

Answers

1. c. The muscles in pattern overload will move about in a certain form, without any variation of how well the muscles can work.
2. b. Nociceptors around the organs will struggle to move signals out accordingly, thus making it harder for the tissues to stay functional.

3. c. The time when a person goes to sleep is not as important as the cycle one enters into or how much time that person spends while asleep, let alone how long it takes for a person to get to sleep.
4. a. An obese patient may use the Rockport walk test to identify how well his or her breathing functions and heart rate may work.
5. a. The MHR is measured by taking 208 and subtracting the product of 0.7 times a person's age. A person who is younger will have a greater MHR thanks to this calculation.
6. d. Pronations may be noticed in the knees and feet when they are moving off-center.
7. d. The circumference test is designed to review the overall size of the body in the midsection by seeing how much of a tape measure goes along the middle.
8. d. While the 1-repetition maximum focuses on strength and the Davies and shark tests concentrate on the body's agility and coordination; the jump test focuses on how well a person can propel his or her body. That is, the effort involves an analysis of a person's ability to use the muscles to shift the body upward.
9. c. While the person should go through the boxes in a clockwise manner, the way a person goes through the boxes is not as critical.
10. a. The short distance between the two cones in the LEFT test will help with identifying how well a person can move between the cones in a few moments.
11. c. The process concentrates mainly on lower body strength and not much on upper body functions.
12. a. A hip joint has to work evenly with the opposite joint.
13. d. Electrodes are needed on the muscles to identify how well they are being worked upon. This may provide a more accurate readout than what one gets from a basic video camera review.
14. c. Excess rotation in the LPHC suggests that the person is favoring a certain part of the body within the workout process.
15. b. A person whose back is straight will be pulling the weight right, without favoring any spots.
16. a. The mass is a total percentage of a part of a person's weight.
17. c. In many cases, a person's lean muscle mass will directly influence how well that person can gain weight. A person with more muscle mass will weigh more, but that weight is healthier in comparison with a person's fat mass.
18. d. The CPT should not try to prescribe any new diet plan.
19. d. A CPT can only diagnose a person with a certain medical condition if that CPT is licensed and certified to produce said diagnosis.
20. d. Each of these may be appropriate times for changing a workout. Cases where someone has dietary changes, based on a nutritionist's recommendation, may also be considered.
21. a. The skinfolds must be tested on this part of the body for a more accurate result.

22. a. A person with pain in the area might elevate or round the shoulders to keep the pain from being too persistent.
23. b. Any measurement between 70 to 80 beats per minute can be interpreted as being healthy.
24. b. The foot may develop overpronation due to the woman having to adjust her feet to handle the dress shoe.
25. d. The knees may not be influenced much due to a person sitting for so long, although the knees should still be reviewing during walking or running tests or activities.

Technique Questions

1. SMR stretching should be avoided if a person:
   a. Has varicose veins
   b. Is pregnant
   c. Has diabetes
   d. All of the above

2. Static stretching should occur at this point in the workout process:
   a. A minute before a workout starts
   b. In the middle of the workout
   c. A few moments after the workout is complete
   d. Near the end of the workout

3. The tempo used in core-training exercises should be planned based on the stage a person is in. For the stabilization stage, the tempo should be:
   a. Gentle
   b. Moderate
   c. Fast
   d. Varied

4. How many reps can be used in a set during a stabilization exercise?
   a. 8
   b. 10
   c. 20
   d. 25

5. When can all planes of motion be used in an SAQ program?
   a. During the stabilization period
   b. In the strength period
   c. During the power process
   d. Throughout the program

6. Isometric contractions may be dangerous during a power stage due to the following:
    a. Limits in what one can lift
    b. The risk of fatigue
    c. A lack of flexibility
    d. Increased irritation in the body

7. Jump-rope exercises can be used in the warm-up process, provided that the following plans are made:
    a. The jump-rope effort should be relaxed
    b. Resistance may be added
    c. A person can jump rope for as long as needed
    d. The speed is fast

8. What should a person do immediately after finishing an extended workout routine?
    a. A light walk
    b. Foam roller support
    c. Extended stretching
    d. Light free weights

9. Is music appropriate for use in kinesthetic training?
    a. Only when appropriate
    b. At all times
    c. Never
    d. If the person chooses the music

10. The Socratic method of discussing what can be done when teaching a workout technique can help with:
    a. Providing very specific details for general use
    b. Planning alternatives for a workout
    c. Filling in ideas
    d. Allowing a person to figure out a solution for his or her technique

11. When can weight be removed from a client's stack?
    a. After a set is finished
    b. While the person is holding the weight before a workout can start
    c. After the client's weight has shifted during a lift
    d. When the person is struggling to keep a full hold over the weight

12. Where should the person's movements be spotted at during a lift?
    a. Hips
    b. Elbows
    c. Knees
    d. Wrists

13. Kinesthetic cueing involves working with the following points:
    a. Telling a person how to handle a technique
    b. Showing a person how to handle the technique
    c. Having a person do something
    d. A and B

14. How long can a cool-down period work for?
    a. 2 minutes
    b. 3 minutes
    c. 7 minutes
    d. 15 minutes

15. When should the number of reps for a set be determined?
    a. Before the start of a session
    b. Before a set begins
    c. While loading weights
    d. Any of these points

16. A person who starts to breathe without using the diaphragm will engage in:
    a. Shallow breathing
    b. Excess breathing
    c. Cyanosis
    d. Kinetic motions

17. A technique works best when there are this many people around the participant:
    a. A spotter and/or CPT
    b. A public space with many people
    c. No other person involved
    d. A small group

18. A kettle bell may be used as part of a workout technique with this intention in mind:
    a. To build core stability
    b. To improve balance
    c. To enhance one's grip strength

d. All of the above

19. A contraindication is a concern in a technique where the exercise may:
    a. Not work without the right equipment
    b. Counteract the effects of another exercise
    c. Cause extreme fatigue
    d. May inhibit one's range of motion

20. When teaching training methods, a person may use the following in the spatial training process:
    a. Videos
    b. Illustrations
    c. Charts
    d. Oral discussion

21. Suspension training is a muscle technique that may be appropriate if:
    a. The weights used are even
    b. The person achieves a certain heart rate in the process
    c. The proper muscles being activated are identified
    d. The weights are not too intense

22. The technique that a senior uses should be planned accordingly, based on:
    a. The type of resistance used
    b. Range of motion
    c. Weights used
    d. Surface for lifting

23. A corrective technique for a workout should involve the following being used for training a person:
    a. Seeing how well individual parts can handle the same amount of weight
    b. Identifying the range of motion
    c. Enhancing flexibility
    d. Improving endurance

24. A foam-rolling technique may be suitable for a workout in the following case:
    a. A person is experiencing inflammation
    b. A muscle appears to be too firm or solid
    c. Proper stretching is needed
    d. A person has tension in certain tissues

25. A super-set technique can include this point for planning timing between exercises:
    a. As little time between two exercises as possible
    b. About two to three minutes between sets
    c. As much time as a person needs for recovery
    d. Only one type of exercise is needed

Answers

1. d. The pressure produced by the rolling motions involved with SMR may be difficult for a patient's body to handle.
2. a. Start the stretching process before the workout to improve how well the body responds to the effort needed.
3. a. A light tempo is needed in the stabilization process to allow the body to become used to the functions that are required in the lifting process.
4. c. 12 to 20 reps should be used in the stabilization process to allow a person to feel comfortable with the workout routine he or she is beginning.
5. c. The sagittal plane should be the only plane utilized in the stabilization process. The user can expand the training routine to include all planes of motion in the later part of the workout, specifically the power point.
6. b. The fatigue that is produced on those muscles may become difficult to support, depending on what you are trying to support.
7. a. The jump-rope effort should be comfortable without being hard to use. You have to maintain a light amount of effort in your work for about five to ten minutes.
8. a. A gentle walk is enough for allowing the body to recover appropriately and to feel comfortable with the workout routine in general.
9. a. Music may be used when someone is aiming to maintain a sense of control over the body, although this is not always required. The trainer should determine if the music is appropriate for the workout session or if it may be distracting or unnecessary in some way.
10. d. This form of teaching technique is designed to help people figure out what they can do when learning about certain things that are suitable for their workout needs.
11. d. Weights can be removed from a stack as a safety measure in the event that someone is unable to handle the weight and is struggling to manage it well enough.
12. d. The wrists should always be analyzed to see that a person is holding a particular series of weights the right way. This is with the intention of seeing that someone can handle the weights appropriately and without risking those weights being dropped incorrectly or otherwise mishandled in some form.

13. c. Although the training technique does entail helping a person to see how something works, this focuses mainly on understanding what can be done with a hands-on approach to the work in question.
14. c. An ideal cool-down period will go from five to 10 minutes. A point in the middle is often ideal for helping a person to feel comfortable about the workout in question.
15. d. The best idea is to get the plan for a number of reps hammered out as soon as possible, although that total may be adjusted based on a person's condition and capacity for handling the weight at a time.
16. a. Shallow breathing may be noticed when a person's breathing functions appear to be far too deep or intense for a person's workout. This could result in substantial breathing issues, depending on what someone can handle at the moment.
17. a. Having a spotter and/or CPT is enough for managing a workout. Having too many people in a space at a time may cause a person to be negatively affected by external influences.
18. d. The design of the kettlebell makes it appropriate for many lifting needs, although proper control over the bell is needed for ensuring the surface is handled right.
19. b. Contraindications are concerns that may make it harder for proper movements to be handled accordingly, although the issue may vary in intensity based on the problem that a person encounters and how challenging the concern might be.
20. c. A chart may provide the person with a clear idea of the techniques that may be required when moving a workout forward.
21. c. An electric stimulation review may be used to identify how well certain muscles are being handled in this part of training, although that review is optional for a person's use.
22. b. A senior's range of motion should be identified carefully based on how well that person can handle the workout routine.
23. b. The range of motion has to improve during the workout routine in order to make it easier for a person to lift weights and to avoid certain problems.
24. d. The rolling mechanism used in this case may help with relieving some tension, but this works best when the process is planned accordingly and ahead of time.
25. a. The super-set process focuses on figuring out how well a person's workout can be handled based on how fast the effort might be and what someone can do to make that process run fast enough.

Program Design Questions

1. In a pyramid set, a person can do the following for a workout:
    a. Keep the same weight in each set

b. Change the lifting process for each set
c. Change the weight used in each set
d. B and C

2. The key part of circuit training is for the exercises in a routine to:
    a. Focus on a specific part of the body
    b. Use the same weight for each exercise
    c. Use the same number of reps and sets on each part of the body
    d. Keep the amount of rest in between each set to a minimum

3. The main point of cardiovascular exercise routines is that a cardiovascular plan will entail:
    a. Extra resistance
    b. A limited range of motion
    c. Changes in breathing
    d. Little to no required equipment

4. Horizontal loading is different from vertical loading in that horizontal loading requires a person to:
    a. Concentrate on one part of the body before going to the next
    b. Use the same amount of weight throughout a routine
    c. Keep the reps and sets for each exercise consistent
    d. Allow for extra rest in between sets

5. The main goal of a power-based routine for a physical workout is to produce:
    a. Faster speed
    b. Added weight
    c. Increased flexibility
    d. Repeated motions many times over

6. The best time to use body-weight-based exercises is:
    a. During the power stage
    b. During the stabilization stage
    c. After adding a certain amount of muscle mass
    d. At the start of a workout routine

7. A person who is struggling to complete the planking exercise can do the following:
    a. Keep the knees on the floor
    b. Allow the elbows to make contact with the floor
    c. Reduce the weight involved

   d. Rest for an extra period

8. The knees-on-the-bridge exercise requires being bent:
   a. To the side
   b. Downward
   c. Upward
   d. No bending needed

9. Core-training exercises may require the following equipment during the power-building process:
   a. Resistance bands
   b. Medicine ball
   c. A reliance on the person's natural body weight
   d. Added stretching

10. The stage that works in between the eccentric and concentric functions in plyometric training involves:
    a. Stabilization
    b. Shifting the body
    c. Amortization
    d. Stretching

11. Box-jumping exercises can be adjusted with:
    a. Changes in the slope on the box
    b. Changes in how far one has to jump to access the box
    c. Any added weights that are added to the person's body
    d. The height of the box

12. The rest period between sets in the stabilization process of a plyometric session should last for this many seconds:
    a. 45
    b. 60
    c. 75
    d. 90

13. For the best result in a steady-state training practice, the workout should be:
    a. At a gentle pace
    b. As fast as possible
    c. Supported with added resistance
    d. Performed in a warm environment

14. The cool-down period should include the following goal:
    a. Keeping the heart rate consistent after the workout is finished
    b. Stretching the body
    c. Getting rest right away
    d. Reducing body temperature

15. As the body goes through the alarm reaction within general adaptation syndrome, the person will experience the release of:
    a. Cortisol
    b. Adrenaline
    c. Growth hormone
    d. A and B

16. A person who develops an inability to continue to work on a specific type of action will experience:
    a. Fatigue
    b. Depression
    c. Burnout
    d. Anxiety

17. The main goal of overload is to allow the body to handle:
    a. More reps and sets
    b. Longer workout routines
    c. Expanded flexes
    d. More weight than what a person might normally be able to handle

18. A cancer patient can use a quick change in the way a workout is planned through the following strategy:
    a. Rest intervals can be longer
    b. Heavy lifting may work
    c. SMR processes help with flexibility
    d. Allow for more reps

19. People with chronic lung illnesses should engage in workouts that entail:
    a. Heavy weights
    b. Light reps
    c. Added rest
    d. B and C

20. The goal of a workout routine for those who have osteoporosis is to:
    a. Strengthen bones

b. Tone muscles
c. Bulk up muscles
d. Increase agility

21. A person who changes body position during a workout may experience this type of change. This should be noticed when reviewing how well the body responds:
    a. Lightheadedness
    b. Blood sugar change
    c. Blood pressure change
    d. Breathing change

22. Stationary bike training is useful in a program designed for:
    a. Pregnant women
    b. Youth participants
    c. People with hypertension
    d. Diabetics

23. It is fine to increase the amount of physical activity in a session among:
    a. Older patients
    b. Younger patients
    c. Pregnant women
    d. People with diabetes

24. What can be done in a case where a senior is struggling to handle a 30-minute exercise routine?
    a. Allow the person to skip a routine
    b. Extended cool-down periods in between sets or exercises
    c. Break the routine into segments to be done throughout the day
    d. Reduce the intensity of the exercises

25. A calorie counter is needed for identifying:
    a. How much is consumed in a day
    b. Specific nutrients
    c. How quickly you consume calories and use them
    d. What foods are right for a workout or routine

Answers

1. c. The weight in each set can be handled with an increase or decrease in weight during each set. A set that entails an increase in weight involves the pyramid moving upward.

2. d. Multiple kinds of exercises may work in circuit training, but the key is to keep the rests in between each set or exercise from being too long. This includes keeping the rest total at about 60 seconds between each set.
3. d. Cardiovascular workouts can include movements that entail the body using its own forces to generate motions. Some resistance may be added to the body during the workout process, but that is optional.
4. a. Horizontal loading sessions may focus on specific parts of the body in one session. The parts that are not handled in that session may be worked upon during the next session.
5. a. The power stage concentrates on using muscles one has already worked out and allows those muscles to become stronger and more durable.
6. a. It is best to work on a body-weight-based process after the muscle gains have been completed.
7. a. The elbows are to support most of the weight in any case, although a person may also keep his or her knees on the floor if necessary.
8. c. The bending process requires the knees to move upward. The person will continue to lie on his or her back.
9. b. Medicine-ball-based exercises are important for allowing the body to respond to certain movements and to work quickly in the lifting process. These exercises include the rotation-chest pass.
10. c. Amortization involves the muscles becoming stable. The muscles will take in more energy so a movement can be completed the right way. The muscle gathers the energy from the eccentric motion and then relieves that energy in the concentric process.
11. c. The positioning and layout of the box should be consistent throughout the routine, although the muscles may use added resistance materials to improve upon how well the body responds to the training process.
12. d. The rest period can be longer in the early stages of the routine, although that total has to go down to 60 seconds during the strength and power portions of the workout.
13. a. The parameters of the steady-state workout will be consistent during the entire workout process. Therefore, the workout should be planned in a gentle manner for the best results.
14. d. While gentle motions are needed during the cool-down period, the main goal is to allow the body to recover to the point where the body temperature will return to normal. Resting right away may only cause harm to the body if not handled appropriately.
15. d. The cortisol that is produced by the adrenal gland will cause adrenaline levels in the body to increase. The condition causes the body's energy stores to rise.
16. c. Burnout can be a significant threat, depending on how well a person can handle the actions managed in the workout effort.

17. d. Adding extra weight makes it easier for the body to handle more motions and movements without any inhibitions. This is vital for a person's general success.
18. a. A patient who has undergone cancer treatments should be allowed to take things lightly during the workout process. This is especially the case for those who have undergone chemotherapy or radiation treatment.
19. d. The weights that a person uses in a routine should be light and should be handled with fewer reps. This is to prevent any possible complications that might develop when trying to lift weights accordingly.
20. b. Muscle tone is critical in the workout process. The bone density issue may be resolved through a healthy diet and with proper medication or supplementation. In this case, an outside dietician needs to be contacted for further help with resolving the concerns the patient might have.
21. c. Blood pressure totals may change as a person adjusts his or her position over time. The blood pressure changes may be particularly concerning among those who have hypertension.
22. a. Although anyone can benefit from stationary bike riding, a pregnant woman will have an easier time getting used to the workout as she focuses more on lighter impacts within her workout.
23. b. Youth participants can handle about 60 minutes of exercise in a day, versus the 30-minute standard that most people utilize.
24. c. The 30-minute period may be changed to allow a person to rest for an extended bit in between each workout session a person employs.
25. d. The calorie counter will help a person with figuring out dietary changes, thus helping that person to make smart decisions.

Nutrition Questions

1. Triglycerides are fatty acids that focus on the following function for storing fats:
    a. Storage
    b. Breakdown
    c. Transfer
    d. Removal

2. Soluble fiber assists the patient in efforts for losing weight and controlling cholesterol levels by:
    a. Being lighter in its texture
    b. Being capable of moving through the bloodstream in a shorter time
    c. Being dissolved in water
    d. All of the above

3. An optimal glycemic index level is:
    a. 40
    b. 50
    c. 60
    d. 70

4. Carbohydrates may be consumed before a workout to:
    a. Increase glycogen stores in the body
    b. Process fiber
    c. Encourage hydration
    d. Promote healthier resting periods with reduced cramping

5. All of these amino acids are considered to be essential amino acids except for:
    a. Lysine
    b. Valine
    c. Serine
    d. Methionine

6. A person's daily caloric content can include this amount of fat, based on the percentage of calories that one consumes at a time:
    a. 15
    b. 25
    c. 40
    d. 50

7. Iron is vital for a healthy workout routine as it does the following for the lungs:
    a. Collects oxygen from the muscles and moves it into the lungs
    b. Moves oxygen from the lungs to the muscles
    c. Triggers natural contraction and expansion functions in the lungs
    d. Tones the muscles around the lungs

8. A person who is looking to lift more weights can consider adding the following micronutrient to his or her diet:
    a. Magnesium
    b. Copper
    c. Selenium
    d. Vitamin C

9. Water may increase the body's metabolic processes, although the water, in this case, needs to be:

a. Cold
b. Pure
c. Consumed consistently throughout the day
d. All of the above

10. A person is looking to take in an hCG diet that entails less than 1,000 calories in a day. What should be done in this case?
    a. Plan a dietary routine for the person to use
    b. Add more fiber to the diet
    c. Increase the amount of water that a person will consume
    d. Refer the patient to a doctor

Answers

1. a. Triglycerides connect to glycerol compounds in the body to support how the body stores fats. These include necessary fats for protecting organs, but some fats may also become excessive and potentially dangerous.
2. c. Most forms of fiber are of the same texture and quality, but soluble fiber is different in that it can dissolve in water.
3. a. Although a good GI level is anything at 55 or lower, the total has to be as low as possible to prevent blood glucose levels from spiking during one's daily routine.
4. a. By consuming 1.5 grams of carbs for every kilogram of weight about 30 minutes before a workout, a person has more energy. The glycogen stores in the body will increase at this juncture, thus supporting healthier functions all the way through.
5. c. Serine is a nonessential amino acid in that the body will naturally produce serine. The essential amino acids are the ones that must be acquired through foods or supplementation as they are not produced within the body on their own.
6. b. The percentage of calories in a day that come from fat should entail 25 to 35 percent of a person's diet. The percentage is needed to maintain proper stability in the body.
7. b. By consuming enough iron in a meal, workouts become easier as oxygen can move into the patient's muscles.
8. b. Although all of the listed micronutrients are effective in helping the body support a strong workout routine, copper is needed for strengthening tendons. This, in turn, improves upon how well the body can handle its natural weight-lifting functions.
9. d. Cold water does a better job with triggering heating functions within the body, thus supporting how well the body can manage natural metabolic functions. Also, cold water should be consumed throughout the day to allow the metabolic process to stay consistent. Added flavorings should be avoided as they may contain more sugars.

10. d. Any patient who is trying to consume a diet with 1,200 calories per day or fewer should talk with a doctor for help. The diet may be risky unless a doctor plans it out accordingly.

Practice Operation and Development Questions

1. You must keep your clients' data private and secure. This includes ensuring that a third party will not handle anyone's details. You must avoid sharing the private details on any clients you have, unless:
    a. You are legally obligated to share the information with someone
    b. The person you are taking care of is a minor, and you need to send this information to parents or a guardian or relative
    c. The person who is working with you directly asks you to share the data
    d. All of the above

2. Liability insurance is needed for keeping your business operational. The insurance policy is for covering issues relating to:
    a. Damages to your work environment
    b. Any repairs for managing equipment
    c. Possible injuries that people experience while in your care
    d. Handling any natural occurrences that may develop

3. Exceptions for efforts may be included in a doctor's clearance note. These may involve:
    a. How often a person can exercise
    b. What exercises a person can do
    c. Medications that may be used
    d. A and B

4. Can you have people work for you as assistants?
    a. Only if you can afford them
    b. Assistants are mandatory
    c. No assistants are needed
    d. Avoid assistants at all costs

5. What can you do when trying to resolve a person's objections to one of your services?
    a. Offer a discount for services
    b. Allow a person to change his or her workout routine

c. Discuss the reasons why a person needs to go through with changes you recommend
d. Allow the person to think about the argument for a day

Answers

1. d. The odds of a client allowing you to give your data to third parties without legal considerations in mind are minimal, but you still have the option to do this if the client says that it is fine.
2. c. Liability insurance ensures that you will cover any medical bills and other damages relating to people who might have been hurt while in your care, for any reason. Such damages can vary in value based on the concerns that someone has.
3. d. You should not have to deal with questions relating to possible medications and treatments. Rather, you need to pay attention to what a doctor says you can do when beginning to work with a person.
4. a. Assistants can help you in many forms for managing your workout administration needs, but you have to ensure you can cover their salaries. These people must also be certified and trained to help people.
5. c. You have to talk with the participant about what makes a workout routine so valuable and essential for a person to follow and utilize.

Client Relations Questions

1. Assertiveness is a necessity for managing a workout. Assertiveness may involve the following:
    a. Planning an interface for a workout
    b. Being direct in explaining what to do in a workout
    c. Understanding pressures and concerns that a person has
    d. All of the above

2. Eye contact should be planned to build rapport with another person in the workout. The eye contact must be:
    a. Casual
    b. Moderate
    c. Intense
    d. Not too focused

3. The main point of producing goals in order to establish rapport is to:
    a. Focus on long-term concepts
    b. Set a time frame
    c. Be realistic
    d. Allow the client to do anything

4. What type of question might be interpreted as a closed-ended question?
    a. What types of exercises have you completed today?
    b. What is your dietary routine of late?
    c. Have you completed the number of sets you were supposed to finish?
    d. What outfit do you have for your workout?

5. The first part of planning a SMART goal involves ensuring the goal being set is specific. This means that the goal has:
    a. A time frame
    b. A very specific intention
    c. A series of steps
    d. All of the above

6. A measurement in a SMART goal may include:
    a. The parts of the body a person wants to work on
    b. The feelings a person has following the workout
    c. Any possibility for a person to grow and thrive
    d. The number of reps that an individual wishes to attain

7. Who can you refer a person to when helping a person with managing stresses?
    a. Physician
    b. Dietician
    c. Yoga practitioner
    d. Friends

8. Who can help a person through external influences that he or she might be struggling with?
    a. Physician
    b. Dietician
    c. Psychologist
    d. Friends

9. The health belief model is a form of behavior that may be exhibited by a client based on that person's:
    a. Enthusiasm
    b. Fear
    c. Productiveness
    d. Curiosity

10. The behavioral model that may directly influence a person's desire to make changes in life is this model:
    a. Self-efficacy
    b. Transtheoretical
    c. Behavioral analysis
    d. Health review

Answers

1. b. Although it helps to suggest things to people and to recognize pressures, assertiveness is about direct discussions while explaining in detail what a person can do in order to have a successful workout.
2. b. Eye contact is needed to show that you will focus on someone, but it is vital for you to keep that eye contact from being far too intense or difficult.
3. c. It is through realism that a client-patient relationship can develop. Being realistic when talking about goals is vital for producing a more useful approach to handling content.
4. c. A closed-ended question is designed to include as few responses as possible.
5. d. Each of these points can be used in the S part of the SMART, goal provided that someone is specific enough. This includes being specific on how long the effort will take, why someone wants to do this and what types of exercises and other fitness-related functions will be utilized in the process.
6. d. Anything that can be measured should be quantified. The other solutions listed here are subjective based on what a person feels may work.
7. c. A yoga practitioner is one of many people that can be contacted regarding managing stresses. A yoga practitioner will help a person to learn what can be done to resolve stresses and pressures throughout the body.
8. c. A psychologist may be hired to help a person manage some of the external stresses and pressures that develop when trying to maintain a healthy routine.
9. b. The health belief model is produced with the belief that a person might develop significant health issues unless an appropriate fitness routine is planned out.
10. b. The transtheoretical model focuses on how someone is willing to make changes in life to succeed and grow while moving forward with the appropriate procedures for managing a workout.

Conclusion

It is through the work of a certified physical trainer that anyone can figure out what must be done to stay healthy and to get the most out of one's body. A CPT will help any person with figuring out how to resolve any physical concerns that one has regarding a workout. The efforts that go into a routine planned by a CPT will help anyone to build muscle mass, produce an appropriate posture and find ways to lose weight. Being a CPT can be very rewarding. It is through your work as a CPT that you will be able to help others who need assistance with getting the most out of their workout routines. You will feel rewarded when you see how well people respond to the training plans that you orchestrate. But for this to work y, you have to show a vested interest in the needs that a person might have when getting a workout up and running.

You must ensure when studying to become a CPT, that you understand what you are getting out of your work. You have to look at what your efforts as a CPT can accomplish while also noting what makes your content outstanding and unique. You have to carefully consider what you are going to do with your participants in your program, in order to make it stand out. You must not only recognize the types of exercises that may be prescribed but also how you are going to have people complete those exercises. This includes an emphasis on how well a person's body can handle certain workouts without struggles.

It is especially important to keep a well-oiled machine going as you keep working hard towards attaining your goals in helping people. You have to not only know what people can do when working out but also recognize the many concerns that someone might have. Be sure to review the points in this guide often and to also find additional information relating to what may come about with the CPT exam in the future. The points relating to the exam are always changing, so it helps to see what you are getting out of the test and how this will work for your plans.

Good luck in your effort with managing the CPT exam and moving forward in your career in this exciting field. Within your work, you will find that it is easy for you to help people with getting more out of their lives, helping them get in shape and feel as strong as possible.

Made in the USA
Middletown, DE
25 April 2020

Developing Godly Character in Children

Sixth Edition

A Unit Study Guide

Beverly Caruso, Ken Marks and Debbie Peterson

Definitions adapted with permission from
Institute in Basic Life Principles
Box One, Oak Brook, IL 60521

ISBN 0-9629038-5-X

Printed in the United States of America

Abba Ministries / Hands to Help Publications
P.O. Box 1388, Lake Elsinore, CA 92532-7325